India

DISCARDED

and

Pakistan

Opposing Viewpoints®

India
and
Pakistan

Opposing Viewpoints®

Other Books of Related Interest

India
and
Pakistan

Opposing Viewpoints ®

William Dudley, *Book Editor*
Laura D. Jenkins, Ph.D., assistant professor of political
science, University of Cincinnati, *Consulting Editor*

Daniel Leone, *President*
Bonnie Szumski, *Publisher*
Scott Barbour, *Managing Editor*
Helen Cothran, *Senior Editor*

OPPOSING
VIEWPOINTS®
SERIES

GREENHAVEN
PRESS®

THOMSON
─────*─────
GALE

San Diego • Detroit • New York • San Francisco • Cleveland
New Haven, Conn. • Waterville, Maine • London • Munich

LIBRARY OF CONGRESS CATALOGING-IN-PUBLICATION DATA

India and Pakistan : opposing viewpoints / William Dudley, book editor.
 p. cm. — (Opposing viewpoints series)
Includes bibliographical references and index.
ISBN 0-7377-1762-9 (lib. : alk. paper) — ISBN 0-7377-1763-7 (pbk. : alk. paper)
 1. Nuclear warfare—India. 2. Nuclear warfare—Pakistan. 3. India—Military relations—Pakistan. 4. Pakistan—Military relations—India. 5. Jammu and Kashmir (India)—Politics and government. I. Dudley, William, 1964– . II. Series.
UA840 .I455 2003
355.02'17'0954—dc21
                 2002034715

"Congress shall make
no law. . . abridging the
freedom of speech, or of
the press."

First Amendment to the U.S. Constitution

The basic foundation of our democracy is the First
Amendment guarantee of freedom of expression.
The Opposing Viewpoints Series is dedicated to the
concept of this basic freedom and the idea that it is
more important to practice it than to enshrine it.

Contents

Why Consider Opposing Viewpoints?

"The only way in which a human being can make some approach to knowing the whole of a subject is by hearing what can be said about it by persons of every variety of opinion and studying all modes in which it can be looked at by every character of mind. No wise man ever acquired his wisdom in any mode but this."

John Stuart Mill

In our media-intensive culture it is not difficult to find differing opinions. Thousands of newspapers and magazines and dozens of radio and television talk shows resound with differing points of view. The difficulty lies in deciding which opinion to agree with and which "experts" seem the most credible. The more inundated we become with differing opinions and claims, the more essential it is to hone critical reading and thinking skills to evaluate these ideas. Opposing Viewpoints books address this problem directly by presenting stimulating debates that can be used to enhance and teach these skills. The varied opinions contained in each book examine many different aspects of a single issue. While examining these conveniently edited opposing views, readers can develop critical thinking skills such as the ability to compare and contrast authors' credibility, facts, argumentation styles, use of persuasive techniques, and other stylistic tools. In short, the Opposing Viewpoints Series is an ideal way to attain the higher-level thinking and reading skills so essential in a culture of diverse and contradictory opinions.

In addition to providing a tool for critical thinking, Opposing Viewpoints books challenge readers to question their own strongly held opinions and assumptions. Most people form their opinions on the basis of upbringing, peer pressure, and personal, cultural, or professional bias. By reading carefully balanced opposing views, readers must directly confront new ideas as well as the opinions of those with whom they disagree. This is not to simplistically argue that everyone who reads opposing views will—or should—change his or her opinion. Instead, the series enhances readers' understanding of their own views by encouraging confrontation with opposing ideas. Careful examination of others' views can lead to the readers' understanding of the logical inconsistencies in their own opinions, perspective on why they hold an opinion, and the consideration of the possibility that their opinion requires further evaluation.

Evaluating Other Opinions

To ensure that this type of examination occurs, Opposing Viewpoints books present all types of opinions. Prominent spokespeople on different sides of each issue as well as well-known professionals from many disciplines challenge the reader. An additional goal of the series is to provide a forum for other, less known, or even unpopular viewpoints. The opinion of an ordinary person who has had to make the decision to cut off life support from a terminally ill relative, for example, may be just as valuable and provide just as much insight as a medical ethicist's professional opinion. The editors have two additional purposes in including these less known views. One, the editors encourage readers to respect others' opinions—even when not enhanced by professional credibility. It is only by reading or listening to and objectively evaluating others' ideas that one can determine whether they are worthy of consideration. Two, the inclusion of such viewpoints encourages the important critical thinking skill of objectively evaluating an author's credentials and bias. This evaluation will illuminate an author's reasons for taking a particular stance on an issue and will aid in readers' evaluation of the author's ideas.

It is our hope that these books will give readers a deeper understanding of the issues debated and an appreciation of the complexity of even seemingly simple issues when good and honest people disagree. This awareness is particularly important in a democratic society such as ours in which people enter into public debate to determine the common good. Those with whom one disagrees should not be regarded as enemies but rather as people whose views deserve careful examination and may shed light on one's own.

Thomas Jefferson once said that "difference of opinion leads to inquiry, and inquiry to truth." Jefferson, a broadly educated man, argued that "if a nation expects to be ignorant and free . . . it expects what never was and never will be." As individuals and as a nation, it is imperative that we consider the opinions of others and examine them with skill and discernment. The Opposing Viewpoints Series is intended to help readers achieve this goal.

David L. Bender and Bruno Leone,
Founders

Greenhaven Press anthologies primarily consist of previously published material taken from a variety of sources, including periodicals, books, scholarly journals, newspapers, government documents, and position papers from private and public organizations. These original sources are often edited for length and to ensure their accessibility for a young adult audience. The anthology editors also change the original titles of these works in order to clearly present the main thesis of each viewpoint and to explicitly indicate the opinion presented in the viewpoint. These alterations are made in consideration of both the reading and comprehension levels of a young adult audience. Every effort is made to ensure that Greenhaven Press accurately reflects the original intent of the authors included in this anthology.

Introduction

"Although the British wisely left their colony peacefully in 1947, the violence that accompanied partition sapped the development of the two states and set the stage for three wars between them."
—Selig S. Harrison, Paul H. Kreisberg, and Dennis Kux

India and Pakistan together account for one fifth of the world's population. Their size and influence have made the continued conflict between them a long-standing cause of global concern. Their adversarial relationship has been marked by three major wars, rival allegiances with other powers (including China, the former Soviet Union, and the United States), many military skirmishes and violent incidents, and a nuclear arms buildup. Both nations trade accusations of meddling in each other's internal affairs and of fomenting violence and civil unrest.

To understand the persistent hostility between these two nations, it is necessary to go back to the circumstances of their modern creation. After centuries in which Hindu, Muslim, and Buddhist rulers had held sway over all or parts of the subcontinent, in the nineteenth century the region became British India, a colony of the British empire. In 1947 Great Britain, weakened by World War II and faced with growing political resistance to British rule, granted independence to its imperial possession. But independence resulted in the birth of not one sovereign nation, but two.

The decision to divide India was made in part because of the insistence of some Muslim leaders within India's movement for self-rule. They became convinced that Muslims could not thrive in a nation in which they would be a minority dominated by Hindus. The "two-nation" theory, espoused by Mohammad Ali Jinnah and other leaders of the Muslim League, held that Hindus, who constituted the majority in most of British India, and Muslims, who constituted the majority only in British India's northeast and northwest corners, should not be forced to live together in one nation, but should each be granted their own country. To safeguard the rights of Muslims, Jinnah and others argued, they must be granted their own state. "Pakistan"—an Urdu-language word meaning "land of the pure"—was coined in the 1930s and became the name of the proposed Muslim nation.

The two-nation theory espoused by the Muslim League was strongly criticized by the Indian National Congress, India's preeminent independence organization (it later became the Congress Party). Its leadership, dominated by Hindus, argued that religion by itself could not constitute the basis for creating either an Islamic Pakistan or a Hindu India. Critics of the two-nation theory noted that Hindus and Muslims had lived side by side throughout the region for centuries before British rule and could not be readily separated. In addition, they asserted that the two-nation theory painted a too-simplistic picture of the divisions that existed within the realm. Not only was it home to millions of adherents of religions other than Hinduism and Islam, it was also the site of diverse ethnic and linguistic groupings that cut across religious lines. Thus, for example, a Muslim could have much more in common with a Hindu who shared a common language and ethnicity than with another Muslim hundreds of miles away with a different language and ethnicity. Indian National Congress leaders, including Mahatma Gandhi and Jawaharlal Nehru, envisioned a unified India under a secular state that would enable people of differing religions, languages, and ethnic groups to coexist. However, while Nehru and others were able to win independence from Great Britain in 1947 and eventually create a secular democratic government in India, they did so at the price of agreeing to the formation of Pakistan.

Great Britain, after negotiating with the Indian National Congress and the Muslim League, eventually agreed to divide India. The parties agreed to establish borders making the northeast and northwest corners of India into a single country with two territories —East Pakistan and West Pakistan—located one thousand miles apart. The process of division itself, called "partition," was an extraordinarily disruptive and destructive event. Millions of people found themselves on the "wrong" side of hastily drawn borders between India and Pakistan. Ten million people moved from one new nation to another. Mob violence accompanying the refugee movement and resettlement—caused by religious conflict that was often stoked by politicians spreading stories of atrocities—cost an estimated one million lives.

India and Pakistan immediately went to war in 1947 over the disputed territory of Kashmir, a thinly populated province between the two nations. The local Hindu *maharaj* (ruler) of Kashmir, given the choice to join either Pakistan or India, chose India despite the fact that its population was mostly Muslim. The war ended with a 1949 cease-fire that left the state of Kashmir split in two, with India ruling the eastern two-thirds of Kashmir while Pakistan gained control of the western third. Kashmir was also the cause of the 1965 war between India and Pakistan; the fighting ended in a military stalemate with the division of Kashmir unchanged.

A third war was sparked not by Kashmir, but by civil conflict within Pakistan itself. East Pakistanis had long complained that Pakistan's government and economy was domi-

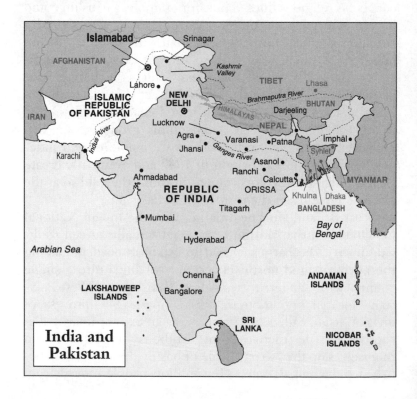

India and Pakistan

nated by West Pakistan. In 1971 India intervened in support of the Aswami League, a political party demanding independence for East Pakistan. The 1971 war resulted in an Indian victory and the secession of East Pakistan from Pakistan to create the new nation of Bangladesh. That result left three nations—Pakistan, Bangladesh, and India—each with roughly 150 million Muslims. Many in India viewed the creation of Bangladesh as a definitive repudiation of the two-nation theory, arguing that Islam, the supposed reason for Pakistan's existence, had failed to hold the country together. But the concept's validity continued to be defended by leaders in Pakistan.

Today, the hostility between India and Pakistan continues to revolve largely around Kashmir. The continuing conflict over which nation should possess Kashmir illustrates how past differences over the two-nation theory continue to underlie current disputes. For Pakistanis (especially its political and military leaders), Kashmir is the "K" in Pakistan—a Muslim-populated territory that by the two-nation theory should be part of the Islamic homeland created in 1947. For many Indians, Kashmir demonstrates that a Muslim-majority state can exist in India—making it a key example of how India brings together people of different faiths. Many Indians believe relinquishing Kashmir would endanger Indian unity. As Indian-born international relations professor Mohammed Ayoob puts it, "Another partition on the basis of religion. . .would reopen the issue of the status of Muslims as Indian citizens and refresh the wounds of partition."

Another legacy of partition and the resulting long-standing hostility between the two nations is the growth and influence of their respective military sectors. Both nations have built up large armies and have developed nuclear weapons primarily to defend themselves from each other. In Pakistan especially, the military has grown so powerful that it has ruled the nation for roughly half of its existence and wielded enormous influence even in times when civilian rulers are nominally in charge. The continued arms race between the two nations has had the unfortunate consequence of impeding the social and economic development of both nations. Many within both countries believe that since both spend great amounts on their military forces, they have underinvested in their people and have committed limited resources to address serious problems such as poverty and pollution.

More than a half century after India and Pakistan gained independence, the ramifications of partition continue to be felt in South Asia. Whether the wounds caused by partition can ever be fully healed is one of many questions facing both nations. *India and Pakistan: Opposing Viewpoints* presents various opinions and analyses from Indian, Pakistani, and foreign scholars and observers in the following chapters: Is Nuclear War Likely Between India and Pakistan? What Is the Status of Human Rights in India and Pakistan? How Should the World Community Treat India and Pakistan? What Lies in the Future for India and Pakistan? The diverse views included in this volume illustrate the multiple challenges faced by these two historically linked yet adversarial nations.

CHAPTER 1

Is Nuclear War Likely Between India and Pakistan?

Chapter Preface

Since their founding in 1947, India and Pakistan have fought major wars in 1948, 1965, and 1971 (the last conflict resulted in the creation of the independent nation of Bangladesh out of what was formerly East Pakistan). In addition, the two countries have clashed almost continuously over Kashmir, a small border region between the two countries. Both countries claim the entire region, which is divided along an international "Line of Control" and which remains the site of occasional military clashes and artillery fire exchanges between the two nations. Pakistan has accused Hindu-dominated India of oppressing Kashmir's people (the majority of whom are Muslim), while India has accused Muslim-dominated Pakistan of sponsoring terrorist and guerrilla forces in the Indian section of Kashmir.

The past history of hostilities between India and Pakistan and the continuing and unresolved dispute concerning Kashmir have become more worrisome to the international community following the development of atomic weapons of mass destruction by both adversaries. India announced in 1974 that it had tested a nuclear device. In 1998 both India and Pakistan exploded nuclear devices in a series of weapons tests. Estimates vary on the number of warheads each country actually has, with India believed to have between fifty and one hundred warheads, and Pakistan from ten to one hundred, according to a 2002 report by the Campaign for Nuclear Disarmament. In addition, both countries have developed and tested guided missiles capable of delivering nuclear weapons across the India-Pakistan border.

Many in the international community fear that hostilities between the two nations over Kashmir may well escalate into a full-blown nuclear conflict. The two countries have "all the ingredients for a nuclear war," according to physicists and peace activists M.V. Ramana (of India) and A.H. Nayyar (of Pakistan). These ingredients include "inadequate precautions to avoid unauthorized use of these [nuclear] weapons" and "leaders who seem sanguine about the dangers of nuclear war." An assessment by America's Defense Intelligence Agency has estimated that such a war could kill 12 million people and injure 6 million more, not including victims of radiation exposure who might die years after the war.

But some observers have argued that it is no coincidence that no major wars have been fought between the two nations since India and Pakistan became nuclear powers. Nuclear war is unlikely, they believe, for the same reason that no nuclear war occurred between the United States and the Soviet Union during the Cold War—the nations' leaders have been and will continue to be deterred from using their nuclear weapons for fear that such use would lead to nuclear retaliation. Indeed, some have argued that nuclear weapons have prevented *conventional* war in the region. "Contrary to . . . media hysteria," writes *Newsweek* editor and foreign policy expert Fareed Zakaria, "nuclear weapons have actually had a sobering effect on both India and Pakistan. . . . Nuclear deterrence is not pretty . . . but it usually works."

The buildup of nuclear armaments in India and Pakistan has generated much analysis and controversy. The viewpoints in this chapter examine the prospects for war and peace in South Asia.

"In the case of India and Pakistan, the outcome [of war simulations] was nearly always catastrophic."

A Nuclear War Between India and Pakistan Is Likely

Sam Gardiner

Sam Gardiner is a retired U.S. Air Force colonel and a visiting professor at the National Defense University. In the following viewpoint, he describes his experiences with war games—simulations carried out by military services and war colleges—that seek to explore what might happen in a real conflict between India and Pakistan. He argues that these "games" are good prognosticators of real events and almost always end in a catastrophic nuclear exchange between India and Pakistan. Gardiner asserts that many Indian and Pakistani leaders still believe it is possible to wage a small conventional conflict and underestimate the risk that such conflict could lead to nuclear war. He argues that the United States cannot do much to prevent nuclear escalation once a war starts, and should instead do more to impress upon India and Pakistan the importance of peace.

As you read, consider the following questions:
1. What statement by an Indian army general does Gardiner find disturbing?
2. What is the most likely place for a war between India and Pakistan to occur, in the author's opinion?
3. Why might Pakistan consider using nuclear weapons on its own territory, according to Gardiner?

Sam Gardiner, "Learn from War Games," *The Washington Post National Weekly Edition*, January 28–February 3, 2002, p. 22. Copyright © 2002 by Sam Gardiner. Reproduced by permission.

"If we have to go to war, jolly good." Those were the words India's army chief, Gen. Padmanabhan, used at a news conference on Jan. 11, [2001,] to describe the prospect of war with Pakistan.

I'm sorry, general. Maybe you were trying to show resolve, or prove that you're tough. But I can tell you from experience, war between India and Pakistan would not be jolly good. It would be very bad.

I've fought in more than 20 "wars" between India and Pakistan. I've seen skirmishes turn into conflagrations. I've seen ferocious attacks across the border, and defending divisions worn down. I've seen Pakistani commanders turn to nuclear weapons to fend off advancing Indian divisions. I've seen New Delhi—a city of more than 11 million—destroyed and hundreds of thousands of its residents killed in a flash. I'm sorry, Gen. Sunderajan Padmanabhan, I've seen nothing that came close to jolly good.

How have I seen these things? In "wars" that took the form of games played out by American war colleges and military services over the past decade—ever since the United States began to seriously worry about the consequences of a clash between India and Pakistan. These are not fanciful intellectual exercises, but serious, two-week-long simulations used to educate American officers, choose weapons systems they will need for the future and better prepare the United States to respond to complex international conflicts. In the past, these "games" have proven to be extraordinarily good prognosticators of events.

Catastrophic Outcomes

In the case of India and Pakistan, the outcome was nearly always catastrophic. And even after the carnage, the fundamental problems dividing the two nations remained unresolved.

In each of the simulated conflicts in South Asia, some incident provoked the two countries into putting their forces into a high state of readiness along their border. Sound familiar? . . .

On the balance sheet, India has a stronger military force. India can field more than a million soldiers; Pakistan around 650,000. For both countries, most of these troops are infantry. But in a major attack, the decisive forces are the armor and mechanized divisions, which have large concentrations of tanks. Although the balance still favors India, in this area the gap is not as great and Pakistan could overcome some of the disadvantage by the wise use of its units.

That means striking quickly, and striking first. To wait is to be at a disadvantage. When it became apparent in the simulations that conflict was inevitable, one of the sides—usually Pakistan—always initiated combat. That's why face-offs such as the current one in 2002 make me extremely nervous.

The historical root and most visible cause of tension between India and Pakistan has been Kashmir, the region controlled by India but claimed by Pakistan as part of its territory. But in previous real-life wars and in the "wars" I've seen, the important fighting doesn't take place in that contested area. The mountains there just don't offer a good place to fight a decisive battle. Both sides look to other parts of the 2,000-mile border that divides them.

The Punjab Valley

The critical terrain for both sides is the Punjab valley, where key north-south roads lie. On the Indian side of the border, these roads are the link to Kashmir. On the Pakistani side, they link the southern part of that country with Lahore and Islamabad. These are strategic lifelines for both nations.

In the earliest games I took part in, before we thought Pakistan possessed nuclear weapons, the conflict tended to move in a relatively benign pattern, based in part on the Arab-Israeli War of October 1973.

I recall a discussion with a colonel on the faculty of the Pakistani defense college who told me that he had his students study that war. I assumed he was interested in how the Israeli army surrounded the Egyptian forces toward the end of the fighting. To my surprise, he said they were interested in Egypt's strategy. They thought it the best example of a weaker country that was defeated in war but achieved its policy objectives.

The lessons of Egypt in 1973 were not lost on Americans playing the role of Pakistani leaders in past years' games. They would engage in some direct fighting, but would also carry out cross-border attacks in areas where Indian forces were not present in strength. It was a take-territory-and-go-to-the-U.N. strategy. It was a pattern repeated from the earlier wars between the two countries.

But war games try to imagine the future, and the U.S. military's view of South Asia's future changed around 1993, when we began to assume that Pakistan would eventually acquire nuclear weapons. (Pakistan did not test a nuclear weapon until spring 1998.) That changed the strategy of the Pakistani leadership. Conventional forces were used differently, and the wars certainly ended differently.

Since then, these war games have unfolded in much more lethal ways. An initial attack by Pakistan generally cuts the

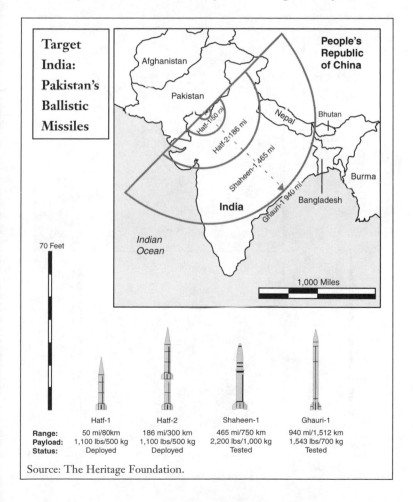

Target India: Pakistan's Ballistic Missiles

	Hatf-1	Hatf-2	Shaheen-1	Ghauri-1
Range:	50 mi/80km	186 mi/300 km	465 mi/750 km	940 mi/1,512 km
Payload:	1,100 lbs/500 kg	1,100 lbs/500 kg	2,200 lbs/1,000 kg	1,543 lbs/700 kg
Status:	Deployed	Deployed	Tested	Tested

Source: The Heritage Foundation.

Indian link to Kashmir. India responds against the Pakistani units in India, but rushes its main forces toward Lahore—Pakistan's second-largest city, and the country's cultural and intellectual center. The Indian teams assume, probably correctly, that, as they advance, Pakistan would be forced to withdraw from its forward positions.

As Indian units advance toward Lahore, which lies just 18 miles from the border post, Pakistan realizes the war is reaching a critical point. If the Indians take the city, they will split Pakistan in two and the Pakistani nuclear weapons will be of little or no use. The Indians must be stopped and must be stopped quickly.

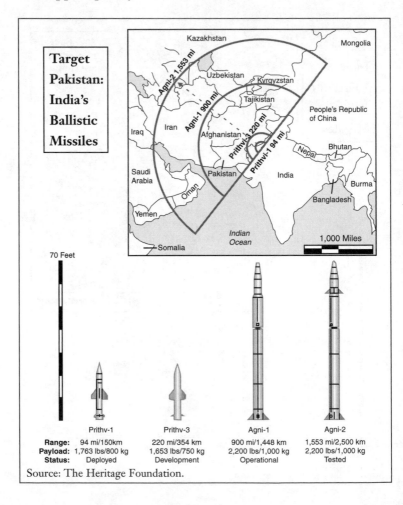

Target Pakistan: India's Ballistic Missiles

70 Feet

	Prithv-1	Prithv-3	Agni-1	Agni-2
Range:	94 mi/150km	220 mi/354 km	900 mi/1,448 km	1,553 mi/2,500 km
Payload:	1,763 lbs/800 kg	1,653 lbs/750 kg	2,200 lbs/1,000 kg	2,200 lbs/1,000 kg
Status:	Deployed	Development	Operational	Tested

Source: The Heritage Foundation.

In our scenarios, the only way for Pakistan to do that is by using nuclear weapons on India's forces inside Pakistan. Strange as that sounds, using nuclear weapons on your own territory has some political advantages, and bears some similarities to NATO [North Atlantic Treaty Organization] strategic options in place during the Cold War. The world would see it as a defensive measure. India would be seen as the aggressor.

It takes three or four nuclear weapons to stop the massive Indian attack. Pakistani forces also suffer heavy casualties from the blasts and radiation, but the Indian advance is halted.

India is left with a dilemma. Does it retaliate against Pakistan with nuclear weapons?

Should it hit Pakistan's cities in its initial strike? That would only further cede the moral high ground to Pakistan. India picks four or five Pakistani military targets for its first use of nuclear weapons, but the attacks also cause significant civilian casualties.

In the simulation, Pakistan responds by dropping a nuclear bomb on New Delhi.

The casualties from this exchange vary depending on the exact targets and the winds, but they would be measured in the millions. If Pakistan drops a relatively primitive nuclear weapon of 20 kilotons, 50 percent of the people living within a one-mile radius of the blast would die immediately. Fires would ignite as far away as two miles, and blast damage would extend to buildings three miles from the point of impact. People 3½ miles away would suffer skin burns and radiation could extend hundreds of miles, depending on the weather.

The participants in these games took no pleasure in unleashing their weapons of mass destruction. To them, it represented failure. In 1998, when India and Pakistan first tested nuclear weapons openly, many strategists said Cold War–style deterrence might prevent war. Yet the danger is that Indian and Pakistani leaders still believe it possible to have a small conventional conflict. Soviet and American leaders didn't think that way during the Cold War. As a result, Soviet and American forces never traded shots across the Iron Curtain the way India and Pakistan have exchanged fire across the Line of Control in Kashmir. NATO and the Warsaw Pact [the Communist states in eastern Europe who signed a mu-tual defense treaty with the Soviet Union] never went to the level of mobilization in Europe that has emerged between India and Pakistan over the past month [January 2002].

What can the United States do? One of the objectives of the war games is to understand how the United States might make a difference, even if it means using our own combat capabilities. After my 20 wars, I still don't know how to do that once hostilities begin. Any use of U.S. forces would mean taking sides; three-sided wars are not possible. The United States would have to side with the weaker party, meaning Pakistan. But that still might not prevent a cataclysmic outcome.

A Better Strategy

A far better strategy would be for the United States to insert itself strongly before armed conflict begins, and get India and Pakistan to realize what they must do. We're not going to quickly solve the underlying problem of Kashmir, but we can press the two sides to stand down, start talking and recognize how easily they can stumble forward to disaster. In the war games, we did not call a timeout and allow the two countries to negotiate. India and Pakistan exchanged messages through their actions. The current cycle might be broken if the United States can bring about a pause for talks.

A few years ago, I ran a war game with my sophomore class at George Mason University. With a little instruction on doctrine and weapons, the two teams managed to fight their way to the all-too-typical results. After the Pakistani team used nuclear weapons on Indian combat formations, I stopped the game and asked them to reflect on the experience.

I heard standard answers. "If we would have moved more divisions to the point of attack, we would have been able to hold out," said one student. "A heavy airstrike as the first move would have changed things," said another. Toward the end of our discussion, one young woman in the class asked a question I've never been able to answer: "Why don't they do this kind of game with the leaders of the countries so they won't let it happen?"

Now that, my dear general, would be a jolly good idea.

> "*It is too early to forget about the psychology and tactics of the Cold War or to dismiss them as part of another . . . era.*"

A Cold War Between India and Pakistan Is Likely

Anne Applebaum

For much of the second half of the twentieth century, the United States and the Soviet Union were in a state of hostilities called the Cold War. Both countries possessed nuclear weapons that were aimed at each other but were never used. In the following viewpoint, journalist Anne Applebaum argues that a similar nuclear standoff, rather than an actual nuclear war, is the most likely scenario between India and Pakistan, both of which possess nuclear weapons. There is no significant reason, she states, to assume that nuclear deterrence would not work to prevent nuclear war between India and Pakistan just as it prevented war between the United States and the Soviet Union. Applebaum is a journalist based in London and Warsaw. Her writings include the book *Between East and West: Across the Borderlands of Europe*.

As you read, consider the following questions:

1. What arguments on why nuclear deterrence will not work with India and Pakistan does Applebaum assess?
2. What arguments concerning India and Pakistan strike the author as being tinged with racism?
3. Is the situation between Pakistan and India dangerous, according to Applebaum?

Presidents [George W.] Bush and Vladimir Putin interrupted their tour of St. Petersburg to warn against it. [Secretary of State] Colin Powell has already been to India and Pakistan to prevent it. Powell's deputy, Richard Armitage, is now heading off to Delhi and Islamabad as well. Yesterday [May 27, 2002] Pakistan promised to respond "with full might" if attacked by India—and today it tested another ballistic missile. But should we really be worried about nuclear war on the subcontinent?

Or perhaps I should put it differently: Is India's nuclear rivalry with Pakistan completely unlike the old nuclear rivalry between United States and the Soviet Union—is it so unique, in fact, that Cold-War-style nuclear deterrence between the two rivals is destined to fail? Consider the arguments as to why it is and it will—or maybe not.

A Common Border

1) India and Pakistan share a common border, along which minor conflagrations might easily turn into a major war—indeed, there has been shelling across the border for some days now. The United States and the USSR did not.

In fact, even though the United States and the USSR did not have a common border, NATO [North Atlantic Treaty Organization] and the Warsaw Pact [the Communist states in eastern Europe who signed a mutual defense treaty with the Soviet Union] shared many common borders, along which there were many minor conflagrations, some of which seemed, at the time, just as likely to develop into nuclear war—the construction of the Berlin Wall and the Berlin airlift, for example.

Confidence-Building Measures

2) The Indians and the Pakistanis have built up fewer confidence-building measures—hotlines and so on. Therefore, the chances of accidents and misunderstandings leading to nuclear warfare are greater.

In fact, the U.S.-USSR hotline—a direct telephone link between the White House and the Kremlin—was created only in 1963. Both before then and after misunderstandings arose constantly. At the height of the Suez crisis in 1956,

NATO radar picked up Soviet aircraft flying over Syria and Turkey. These turned out to be a routine escort for the Syrian president and a flock of swans, respectively. At the height of the Cuban missile crisis, a Soviet satellite accidentally exploded, leading the United States briefly to believe the USSR had launched a massive missile attack. Similar incidents were far more frequent than is usually realized . . . yet none actually did lead to nuclear war.

Borderline Racist Arguments

3) The Indians and the Pakistanis have less experience with nuclear weapons and do not fully understand the consequences of a nuclear war.

This argument, which strikes me as borderline racist, appeared in the British *Guardian* newspaper, of all places. "The trouble is," a South Asia military analyst told the paper, "both sides imagine that a nuclear bomb just makes a bigger bang. They have got no concept of the sheer magnitude of the disaster of a nuclear exchange. Radioactive fallout in the Himalayas would mean the death of the subcontinent." But presumably, if India and Pakistan are technologically sophisticated enough to build bombs, then at least their scientists are technologically sophisticated enough to understand the environmental consequences of the bomb. Indeed, some Indian scientists now lobby against the bomb; so do antinuclear movements in both India and Pakistan. Perhaps only a relatively tiny elite understands the full consequences—but only a tiny elite makes decisions about whether to drop bombs anyway.

4) The Indians and the Pakistanis are crazier than the Americans and the Soviets (this argument, an extension of the previous one, is usually put more delicately, but you know what I mean).

To this there is one response: Richard Nixon. He may have conducted a diplomatic breakthrough in China, he may have known a thing or two about foreign policy, but the man was mad as a hatter. As this is not the time and place to dicuss his paranoia or his inferiority complexes, I will leave you with one salient fact about him: From time to time, Nixon would suddenly put U.S. forces around the world on

The assumption that it's lunacy for nuclear-armed powers to threaten each other is groundless. During the Cold War, American presidents often found it useful to convey to the Soviets our willingness to go to war. Sometimes that meant taking the risk of a Soviet nuclear strike (as in the Cuban missile crisis) and sometimes it meant threatening to launch a nuclear strike (an option we held out in case of a Soviet attack in Europe).

But in each case, the missiles stayed in their silos. The Indians and Pakistanis are doing the same thing, and they're not likely to end up using their nukes either. Nuclear deterrence worked in the Cold War, and it should work in South Asia.

Stephen Chapman, *Conservative Chronicle*, June 19, 2002.

high-security alert, scramble the planes, ratchet up the coded transmissions just to keep the Soviets on their toes. Crazy, yes—but even he managed not to destroy the world.

Language and Deterrence

5) Pakistani President Pervez Musharraf has begun to use very threatening language. "We do not want war," he said yesterday [May 27, 2002], "but if war is thrust upon us, we would respond with full might."

In fact, threats are as essential to effective nuclear deterrence as the missiles themselves, and we shouldn't necessarily be put off by them. Indeed [Soviet leader Nikita] Khrushchev's boasts about the USSR's (nonexistent) nuclear prowess actually convinced the United States, at one point, of the existence of a "missile gap." In the current conflict too, saber-rattling has its uses: If India really believes Pakistan will fight back with nuclear weapons, then it will be less likely to launch a full-blooded invasion of Pakistan in the first place. Pakistan's ballistic-missile testing falls in the same category: It might prevent war just as easily as it might encourage war.

A Balance of Terror

6) The Indian nuclear arsenal is larger, and the Pakistanis do not pose a credible counter-threat. The Indians might therefore be tempted to use their nuclear weapons first.

At the moment, the Indian army, which is far bigger than the Pakistani army, is committed to a no-first-use policy. India would, by all accounts, win any conventional war rather quickly, so it has no need to use nuclear weapons first. In any case, estimates of India's "prowess" range widely (from 40 to 250 warheads) as do estimates of the Pakistani nuclear arsenal (from 20 to 150 warheads). What matters, again, is not the sheer numbers, but that both sides fear that the other can inflict huge damages. The projections—12 million dead on the first day of nuclear exchange—are indeed huge and should be enough to make both sides think twice. That is the admittedly insane essence of deterrence: a "balance of terror."

7) Even so, the United States and the USSR went to the brink of nuclear conflict several times, just barely managing to avoid it. Why should we be so certain that the various accidents and flukes and misunderstandings won't have a different outcome this time?

We shouldn't—which is why the situation remains very, very dangerous. My point, in writing all this, is not to deny the hazards of the current South Asian hostilities or to downplay what would be a horrific tragedy if the conflict did come to nuclear exchange. My point is merely that it is too early to forget about the psychology and tactics of the Cold War or to dismiss them as part of another, more irrational era. They are going to be used again—and so far, there is no evidence that Indians and Pakistanis will behave any more irresponsibly than we so often did ourselves.

"There are no worthy arguments for nuclear weapons."

Nuclear Weapons Decrease India's and Pakistan's Security

Praful Bidwai

Praful Bidwai, former senior editor of the *Times of India*, is a writer whose work has appeared in numerous American and Indian publications. He is a cofounder of the Movement in India for Nuclear Disarmament (MIND). In the following viewpoint, he argues that, contrary to the optimistic predictions of some, nuclear weapons have not given India and Pakistan greater international prestige and security. Such weapons have instead made relations between the two nations more strained as each outbreak of conflict threatens to escalate into a nuclear exchange. He concludes by calling for India and Pakistan to rid themselves of nuclear bombs.

As you read, consider the following questions:

1. What promises did Pakistani and Indian experts make regarding nuclear weapons in 1998, according to Bidwai?
2. How do nuclear weapons degrade India and Pakistan's security, according to the author?
3. How close did India and Pakistan come to using nuclear weapons in 1999, in the author's view?

When India detonated five nuclear bombs four years ago [in 1998], many of its leaders, especially BJP [Bharatiya Janata Party] ministers, convinced themselves that New Delhi had now staked an irrefutable claim to both international prestige and security. When [Pakistani prime minister] Nawaz Sharif set off six of his own blasts in "retaliation", he boasted: "Ab Pakistan hamesha ke liye mahfooz ho gaya." (Now Pakistan has become safe forever.)

Optimistic Projections

Strategic "experts" in both countries duly spun out fanciful ex post rationalisations for the blasts. India and Pakistan, they prophesied, would both become more secure. "Maturity" and sobriety would be infused into their fraught relationship. South Asia would become "stable". India and Pakistan would gain in global stature and expand their room for independent manoeuvre.

And of course, as the theory of nuclear deterrence ordains, India and Pakistan, being nuclear powers, would never go to war again. Their leaders, however reckless, would be compelled to realise that even conventional war is unacceptably risky. Doesn't deterrence theory tell you that? The US and the USSR didn't exchange a single shot during the Cold War.

Today, all these predictions stand demolished—many times over. The hope that India and Pakistan would behave with "maturity" lies in tatters as they confront each other with more than a million troops, but without a clearly defined political purpose. The barbaric [May 14, 2002] Jammu terrorist attack [against an Indian army camp] has further aggravated matters. New Delhi blames it on Pakistan-sponsored militants.

"Limited strikes" by India seem imminent. So does "retaliation" by Pakistan, leading to a full-scale conventional conflict. Indian and Pakistani leaders may well bend to the inexorable logic of action-reaction, escalate that conflict to the nuclear plane, and thus finally disprove deterrence theory—with catastrophic consequences for their peoples.

Four years on, it should be plain that nuclear weapons have failed to deliver to India and Pakistan any of the "beneficial" things they were meant to give. But they have fulfilled the most dismal of pessimistic projections.

I personally plead guilty to some such projections. A year after [India and Pakistan tested nuclear weapons in 1998], Achin Vanaik and I co-authored "South Asia on a Short Fuse: Nuclear Politics and the Future of Global Disarmament" (since published by Oxford University Press, Karachi), in which we argued that nuclear weapons would degrade India and Pakistan's security.

In India, we said, they would disastrously strengthen the forces of Hindutva nationalism, militarism, and communalism. Their strategic, social, economic, and political costs would prove onerous.

Danziger. © 2002 by Jeff Danziger. Reprinted with permission.

On Pakistan, our analysis was even more sombre: "In . . . retrospect, [nuclearisation] might well be seen as the final act that precipitated a decisive historical transformation of the Pakistan polity, dramatically reversing for a long time to come the difficult process of democratic consolidation. One hopes this will not be the case, but it could be . . .

"The systemic crisis of legitimacy, the increasing loss of the state's moral purpose, the inability of Islam to provide the foundations of a viable state, have all contributed to the growing failure of the Pakistani political system. . . . If Pakistan proceeds to manufacture and deploy nuclear weapons . . . , the economic consequences could become unbearable . . ."

Regrettably, these forecasts have largely materialised. A particularly corrosive consequence of nuclearisation, mediated by the 1999 Kargil war [a conflict begun when Pakistani-led troops entered Kargil in India-controlled Kashmir, but withdrew after eight weeks of fighting against Indian forces], has been Pakistan's greatly deepened crisis of governance. Pakistan got a major break because of [President] Pervez Musharraf's decision to execute a U-turn on his Afghan policy and join the US' "war on terrorism" [following the September 11, 2001, terrorist attacts on America]. Musharraf took some action against jihadi fundamentalists, haltingly and hesitantly. But the recent downslide in this is only too obvious.

A Horrific Story

To return to Kargil, it has turned out a more horrific story than we all imagined. In a sensational report, *The Sunday Times* (London) has revealed that the Pakistani army mobilised its nuclear arsenal against India during that war without the knowledge of Prime Minister Nawaz Sharif.

Citing Bruce Riedel, a senior White House adviser, the story says that US intelligence had gathered "disturbing information," suggesting India and Pakistan "were heading for a deadly descent into full-scale conflict, with a danger of nuclear cataclysm".

Although Riedel is silent on India's counter-preparations, it is almost inconceivable that New Delhi would not have drawn up plans for using nuclear weapons.

Sharif was told the truth about Pakistan's nuclear preparations by former President Bill Clinton, in Washington. Pakistan's army tightly controls all information about nuclear activities—to the point of keeping the civilian leadership in the dark. Earlier, Benazir Bhutto too had to beg the CIA to brief her on Islamabad's nuclear capability. Her own army denied her that—when she was prime minister!

When reminded by Clinton of how the US and the USSR

had come close to nuclear war over Cuba in 1962, an "ex-hausted" Sharif recognised the "catastrophic" danger, and "said he was against [the preparations], but worried for his life back in Pakistan". This prepared the ground for an end to the Kargil conflict—much to Musharraf's annoyance.

The rest is history. [In October 1999 Pervez Musharraf, Pakistan's army chief of staff, overthrew Prime Minister Nawaz Sharif in a bloodless coup.]

This gives a hair-raising edge to the well-founded fears expressed by many analysts, including me, that the Kargil conflict had a dangerous nuclear-escalation potential. I once counted that India and Pakistan exchanged nuclear threats no fewer than 13 times during that seven weeks–long war—itself the world's biggest-ever conventional conflict between two nuclear-weapons states.

The disclosure that we were on the brink of a nuclear catastrophe in 1999 should chill many spines. In nuclear war, it doesn't take two to tango. A single adventurist move can have catastrophic consequences for millions of people. Wreaking nuclear devastation upon the adversary after he has used a nuclear weapon against you can only be an act of mindless revenge, not of regaining your security.

Such a dangerous stand-off may again be imminent. Pakistan and India have not only failed to evolve a stable deterrent equation. They probably cannot do so. Nuclear weapons will always be a strategic liability for them. India's rulers are discovering that time and again.

As for Pakistan, nuclear weapons figure in Musharraf's January 12 [2002] address as a constraint, as something to be guarded and protected, not as a means with which to negotiate Washington's demand to "cooperate" with its Afghan operation [in America's war against terrorism].

So much for nukes expanding your room for independent policy-making or giving you a greater voice in the world!

No Argument for Nuclear Weapons

Nuclear weapons have failed to bestow great power status upon India too. India's profile has recently risen in the US more because of Silicon Valley immigrants [Indian immigrants to America that have attained prominent success in the software industry] than because of factors intrinsic to India, and in spite of nuclear weapons. . . .

There are no worthy arguments for nuclear weapons. There are many strong ones for ridding South Asia of these instruments of genocide. The strongest one comes from the grave threat of annihilation which they pose to millions of us non-combatant civilians.

South Asia will remain the world's most dangerous place so long as it has nuclear weapons—the globe's only region where two strategic rivals remain locked in a continuous hot-cold war for half a century, and where countless disputes and events can suddenly precipitate a terrible crisis with an escalation potential.

To become even minimally secure, South Asia must come out of the Bomb's dark shadow.

"If India and Pakistan were not nuclear powers, there is a good chance they would now be at war."

Nuclear Weapons Have Increased India's and Pakistan's Security

Matthew Parris

In 2002 many feared that war would break out between India and Pakistan over the disputed territory of Kashmir as troops from both countries were mobilized and the country's leaders issued threats of attack. In the following viewpoint, Matthew Parris argues that the possession of nuclear weapons by both sides prevented this state of hostilities between India and Pakistan from erupting into war. War between India and Pakistan would be far more likely if neither possessed nuclear arms, he contends. In addition, he asserts that nuclear weapons have given both India and Pakistan greater attention and deference from the United States and other nations. Parris is a political columnist for the London *Times* newspaper.

As you read, consider the following questions:

1. What two levels of argument can be used to support nuclear weapons, according to Parris?
2. What scenarios does the author envision might happen if neither Pakistan nor India had nuclear bombs?
3. How have nuclear weapons affected the way other countries treat India and Pakistan, according to Parris?

Two cheers for weapons of mass destruction. If India and Pakistan were not nuclear powers, there is a good chance they would now be at war. I can think of no clearer practical illustration of the case for the possession of an atomic bomb than the chapter of modern history which has just unfolded in the subcontinent.

As a helpful example it is stronger than the United States' nuclear attack on Japan at the end of the second world war. That attack probably shortened the war and led to a net reduction in the number of lives which would otherwise have been lost. But over Kashmir there was no need for even a limited admonitory strike by either side. There was no strike at all. The threat alone defused the situation. No lives were lost. This was always the classic case for nuclear weapons, and it has just been demonstrated.

Two Levels of Argument

Support for the nuclear argument is offered on two levels: first, from the selfish and separate point of view of each of the potential belligerents, each may conclude that they would have been attacked—with conventional or with nuclear weapons—if they had not themselves had the capability to respond with a nuclear strike.

If Pakistan had no nuclear weapons, the Pakistanis would have been at a disadvantage. India is the superior power in conventional terms. Without Pakistan's nuclear capacity, that country might have expected a brutal and swift incursion by conventional Indian forces, to seek out and destroy the camps where India suspects that Islamic terrorists hide and train for cross-border operations in Kashmir [a border territory both India and Pakistan claim]. Islamabad must conclude that its nuclear missiles probably saved the nation from such an Indian operation.

If Pakistan had been a nuclear power, but not India, the Indians would surely be right to fear that Islamabad could afford to be careless of Indian protests about terrorist activity in Kashmir, which would almost certainly be carried on more boldly and perhaps with the open connivance of Islamabad. New Delhi must conclude that its nuclear capacity is helping deter such open meddling by Pakistan.

It follows that in neither country can CND [the Campaign for Nuclear Disarmament, a British organization] expect much of a hearing at present. Both, for their different reasons, must feel that their weapons of mass destruction are shielding them from aggression.

This much is obvious. Nevertheless it is possible in game theory for each individual player in a group to protect his own best advantage, yet for this to engender a situation which is not optimal for the group as a whole. Small firearms may be a case in point: if others are to have small firearms, it is probably best that we have them too; but best of all would be for nobody to have them. Were this true in the nuclear case, it would argue for universal nuclear disarmament, by mutual consent or at the command of a power superior to all.

But is it true? Were we in the position to strip both potential combatants in this case—India and Pakistan—of their nuclear weaponry, would the subcontinent be a safer place? I think the anti-nuclear lobby would find it hard to make a convincing argument that this is so.

A Sobering Effect

Contrary to much of the media hysteria, nuclear weapons have actually had a sobering effect on both India and Pakistan. In the first 30 years of their independence (pre-nukes) they fought three wars; in the second 30 (post-nukes) they have fought none. To put it another way, if neither side had nuclear weapons, they would be at war right now. Nuclear deterrence is not pretty—remember the Cuban missile crisis—but it usually works.

Fareed Zakaria, *Newsweek*, June 10, 2002.

The closest approach I can make to such an argument is to maintain that, India being the richer and more populous power and therefore always likely to have the military edge over Pakistan, the Pakistanis would have been deterred long ago from offering any provocation at all; fearful of a conventional strike by India they would have dealt decisively with the extremist Islamic terrorists who use their country as a base, and dropped their covert support for Kashmiri separatists. On this argument it is Pakistan's nuclear capability which, equalising the balance, has given Islamabad Dutch courage.

But I think it is optimistic to suppose either that Pakistan has the ability, if she wished it, to close down the Kashmiri separatist movement, or that she would necessarily wish it anyway—despite India's strength. History offers many examples of long-running, low-level harassment of stronger states by weaker ones. Furthermore, in a situation where each side's belief in the good faith of the other is so weak, there would always be scope for misunderstanding. Pakistani governments might do all they could to contain their extremists, and still not satisfy New Delhi.

I conclude—and even those who disagree would accept that this is very arguable—that an all-conventional subcontinent would be a dangerous and unstable place, and that the clear conventional superiority of India would not itself lead to peace.

The Nuclear Balance

The nuclear balance just has. Credit for the abrupt détente of recent weeks [in June 2002] has been variously awarded to India, to Pakistan, to America, or to all three. It is all three. [Indian prime minister] Atal Bihari Vajpayee showed, in the end and after some sabre-rattling, restraint in accepting Pakistan's good faith in its attempts to clamp down on cross-border terrorism. General [Pervez] Musharraf showed courage in making them. The United States showed not just skill but urgent determination to help, by forcefully counselling peace, to advance it. Washington acted, said the *Times*, 'with calm and brutal insistence'.

Well Washington would, wouldn't they? Russia helped. So did Britain and Europe. It is hard to believe that the world would have moved so fast or so forcefully if a nuclear catastrophe would not otherwise have looked possible.

Yet both potential combatants, India and Pakistan, can emerge content that this was their détente on their mutual terms: no great third power has forced either party into an unequal truce. No great third power dare. It is hard to believe that either India or Pakistan could have expected outside involvement to have been so respectful to each, as in the event it was, had not both been nuclear powers.

In the second half of the last century an effective stand-off between two great nuclear powers bought, paradoxically, a good measure of independence for myriad smaller powers who were military minnows by comparison. That balance has gone. There is now only one great power in the world, and she is a nuclear power. What fear can she feel for other nation-states and their little armies? Towards whom can she now feel any kind of nervousness, except those smaller nations who have, or are rumoured to have, nuclear weaponry?

In this new world only two means of defence now retain their potency: the most sophisticated and the least: nuclear war and terrorist nuisance: destruction and attrition.

*"Washington has a moral responsibility to
undo the crisis in South Asia."*

The United States Must Intervene to Prevent Nuclear War Between Pakistan and India

Muqtedar Khan

In the following viewpoint, Muqtedar Khan argues that the United States shares some of the responsibility for India's dangerous provocations against Pakistan that might cause a nuclear war. America's rhetorical and military war on terror following the September 11, 2001, attacks against New York and Washington have encouraged India to consider a similar military response against terrorists and fighters in the disputed territory of Kashmir. He argues that the United States has the responsibility to actively intervene between India and Pakistan and convince both sides to resolve their differences at the negotiating table. Khan is a professor of politics at Adrian College in Michigan. His writings include the book *American Muslims: Between Faith and Freedom*, academic articles, and syndicated columns on both global and Islamic affairs.

As you read, consider the following questions:

1. What domestic reasons do India's leaders have for threatening war against Pakistan, according to Khan?
2. What goals does the author outline for U.S. policy makers with regard to India and Kashmir?
3. What must Pakistan do to preserve peace, in Khan's view?

Muqtedar Khan, "India Flirting with Disaster," *Foreign Policy in Focus, Global Affairs Commentary*, June 5, 2002, pp. 1–2. Copyright © 2002 by Interhemispheric Resource Center (IRC). Reproduced by permission.

India is playing a highly risky game of brinkmanship in Kashmir. Its 2002 deployment of forces along the line of control (LoC), the *de facto* border between India and Pakistan in Kashmir, and the extremely provocative rhetoric from Delhi have brought the region closer to a nuclear war than ever before.

India is probably betting that it can use the new international environment created by the American campaign against terror in the aftermath of [the September 11, 2001, terrorist attacks on America] as a window of opportunity to not only suppress the Kashmiri uprising, but to also punish Pakistan for supporting and aiding the Kashmiri cause.

Its geopolitical gamesmanship notwithstanding, India does not want a war. Its leaders and most of its population understand that this is a war that they cannot win. India, which has a 3:1 advantage over Pakistan in conventional forces, a 7:1 advantage in manpower, and nearly a 10:1 advantage in economics, can easily overwhelm Pakistan in a conventional war. Both nations are aware of this fact. This reality implies that in order to defend itself Pakistan must immediately resort to nuclear weapons at the onset of war. Sure India will respond, and will probably wipe Pakistan from the map, but with it will go Bombay, maybe Delhi, and much of the population of Western and Northern India. While India may destroy Pakistan, it is highly unlikely that India will politically survive the conflict. It will most probably fragment into a failed state like Somalia. Its triumphant citizens, already poor, will be struggling with even greater poverty, as well as radiation and environmental problems.

Most people are aware of the devastating possibilities that I have sketched. So why, all of a sudden, is India acting so belligerently and risking disaster? There are two reasons why India is indulging in this dangerous game.

Domestic Politics

India has expressed outrage about the recent deaths of civilians in the conflict zone, where sadly the loss of innocent lives is routine. But such outrage serves to distract public attention from the massacre in Gujarat earlier this year. In March [2002], the Bharatiya Janata Party (BJP) government, which rules at the Federal level, orchestrated a brutal massacre and arson of nearly three thousand of its own citizens in Gujarat, a state that it also governs.

In the past two months [since March 2002], India's ruling party has been the target of international outrage and condemnation for its involvement in and mishandling of the Gujarat massacre. The domestic press as well as the international press was carrying story after story of government complicity in the massacre of Muslims in Gujarat, before and after the tragedy. The BJP—which had lost several regional elections in 2001—needs a . . . [distraction] to take away the focus from its failure in Gujarat and rally the nation behind it. The prospect of war with archenemy Pakistan is the answer to BJP's domestic woes.

U.S. Rhetoric on Terror

The second reason is the new environment fostered by Washington's diplomatic and rhetorical war on terror. Encouraged by Washington's attitude of sacrificing rights and trampling democracy (at home and abroad) in its "war on terror," nations like India and Israel now feel emboldened to use force and the threat of force to suppress legitimate struggles for freedoms. . . . The Israeli incursions into the West Bank . . . are a direct consequence of America's rhetoric about fighting terror. India's brinkmanship that at present threatens a nuclear war, which could lead to hundreds of millions of deaths in the region and a global environmental catastrophe, may well be the next consequence. The thinking in Delhi is that if the U.S. and Israel can use military force in response to terror, then why can't India? If Israel can enter the West Bank and the U.S. can occupy Afghanistan, then why cannot India cross the line of control in Kashmir?

This means very simply that Washington has a moral responsibility to undo the crisis in South Asia. A crisis that has emerged because Delhi has been emboldened by Washington to act like Washington.

Steps to Peace

There are two goals that Defense Secretary [Donald] Rumsfeld must pursue during his forthcoming [June 2002] visit to

South Asia. Firstly he must try to ensure that India does not cross the actual line of control. He must convince India that Washington's rhetoric on terror is not a license to begin nuclear conflicts.

U.S. Steps

The United States may find itself in the singularly unenviable position of having to choose between an uncertain but necessary ally, Pakistan, and a long-term potential strategic partner and democracy, India.

The most immediate interest of the United States, clearly, is to forestall and ideally prevent another war between India and Pakistan. In all likelihood, U.S. pressure on both capitals will lead the two states to step away from the brink. Then the United States must do two things: It must forcefully persuade Pakistan to eschew support for the Islamic militants in Kashmir and simultaneously convince India that a lasting peace can emerge only if the genuine grievances of the Muslim population in the Kashmir Valley are adequately addressed. Adopting these two negotiating principles will be neither easy nor painless. But for India and Pakistan, there is no other path away from the precipice.

Sumit Ganguly, *American Prospect*, July 1, 2002.

He must also take steps to prevent accidental war initiation. This will require not only diplomatic efforts but also sharing satellite intelligence about troop movements at the LoC to let the two nations have real time knowledge of each other's troops. Secretary of Defense Rumsfeld could also suggest the introduction of international monitors (perhaps under UN purview) to patrol the LoC. Such a force will not only separate the two forces, but will also effectively seal the border and stem cross-border activities by Jihadi and Kashmiri militants.

Secondly, Washington must brush aside India's refusal to allow American involvement and immediately bring the two nations to the negotiating table. The object of these talks would be to convince India to resolve the Kashmir issue democratically and in compliance with international laws and resolutions. At least some positive steps in this direction must be taken by India, which would give Kashmiris the hope that talks and not tanks will serve their cause.

Jihadis Must Be Dismantled

Pakistan must reciprocate by quickly and effectively putting the Jihadis [Pakistan-based Islamic militants] out of business. These groups are a national security threat to both India and Pakistan and a grave danger to the future of the region. The Jihadi groups are determined to cause trouble. They are trying to destabilize [Pakistan president Pervez] Musharraf's government. The . . . attacks in Kashmir are their revenge against Musharraf for his U-turn when the U.S. demanded Pakistani cooperation in operation Enduring Freedom [America's 2001 campaign against Afghanistan]. India's saber rattling only aggravates the situation. It weakens Musharraf and exaggerates the impact of the Jihadis. It is imperative that India and the U.S. push to assist Musharraf in neutralizing the Jihadis' influence and capabilities

Pakistan has very few options really. Either it risks a civil war by aggressively disarming the militants that operate out of Pakistan, or it risks an unlimited nuclear war with India. If Pakistan cannot control activities within its own borders, then it must let India cross the LoC and do the job.

President [George W.] Bush probably never anticipated that fighting a war on terror entailed peacekeeping in the most troublesome of neighborhoods. This time it is South Asia that interrupts his crusade, demanding his services as a peace broker.

*"There has been no concerted international
effort to . . . prevent a nuclear exchange
that would kill millions in both countries."*

The United Nations Must Intervene to Prevent Nuclear War Between Pakistan and India

Charles Glass

Charles Glass is an American journalist and a former Middle East correspondent for ABC News. In the following viewpoint, he argues that the United Nations has the legal and moral obligation to intervene in India and Pakistan's dispute over Kashmir in order to prevent the two nations from waging a nuclear war. The United States by itself can do little, he argues, but the world's countries working together under the international body can help resolve the Kashmir dispute. Glass argues that the United Nations risks a repetition of its failure to prevent the 1994 Rwanda genocide that produced hundreds of thousands of casualties.

As you read, consider the following questions:
1. According to Glass, what articles of the United Nations Charter authorize it to intervene in Kashmir?
2. What does the author recommend should be done about Kashmir?
3. Who does Glass blame for the Rwandan genocide?

India and Pakistan are at war. A million troops stand mobilised on either side of the 1972 line of control that separates the two countries in Kashmir. Civilians on both sides are dying in artillery exchanges. Pakistani-armed militants have attacked Indian troops and civilians in India. Pakistan and India have, by international consensus, at least 200 nuclear warheads between them. If ever the United Nations Security Council had the obligation to invoke Article 34, calling for investigation of disputes 'likely to endanger the maintenance of international peace and security', this must be it.

So what is happening at the UN? An emergency session, urgent discussions, formation of a peacekeeping force, proposed sanctions for the two parties if they escalate the conflict? Not exactly. A Reuters report conveys the urgency: 'Security Council members agree India and Pakistan's dispute over Kashmir should be left to bilateral diplomatic efforts outside of the UN, Syrian Ambassador Mikhail Wehbe said on Tuesday' [June 4, 2002].

The UN is abdicating its legal role. In its place, bilateral diplomacy permits the threat of nuclear war to grow. The UN Charter allows any state (Article 35) or the Secretary General (Article 99) to place any threat to international peace before the Security Council.

No one has done so. Instead, the United States has sent a Deputy Secretary of State, Richard Armitage, and is sending Defence Secretary Donald Rumsfeld to discuss the conflict with the leaders of Pakistan and India. The Russian President, Vladimir Putin, has invited Pakistani President Pervez Musharraf and Indian Prime Minister Atal Behari Vajpayee to Moscow. Britain has sent emissaries.

But there has been no concerted international effort to end the latest small-scale war or to prevent a nuclear exchange that would kill millions in both countries. The five permanent members of the UN Security Council, Britain among them, are not invoking international law to protect civilians from what will be a genocide.

Limits of American Diplomacy

American diplomacy is having as much effect on India as President George Bush's admonition to Israeli Prime Minister Ariel Sharon earlier this year to withdraw his forces from Palestinian territory 'immediately', 'at once' and 'without delay'. If Bush cannot influence a country that the US subsidises with more than $3 billion a year, why should the Indians and Pakistanis listen to him? If the US has no influence, what can little Britain or emasculated Russia do? At the UN, the US, Russia, China and the rest of the world could work together to force an agreement on two leaders who fear losing face more than they fear the destruction of their countries.

Article 34 of the United Nations Charter

The Security Council may investigate any dispute, or any situation which might lead to international friction or give rise to a dispute, in order to determine whether the continuance of the dispute or situation is likely to endanger the maintenance of international peace and security.

Charter of the United Nations.

Security Council resolutions of 1947, 1965, 1971 and 1972 established a framework for resolving the dispute over Kashmir. The UN Military Observer Group in India and Pakistan, first deployed in 1949, remains in position to become a larger, stronger force that could help both sides to police the border. Pakistan must prevent infiltration of India and close its insurgent bases. India should be made to respect UN resolutions calling for a referendum in Kashmir. Britain's India Act of 1947 gave the Kashmiris the right to choose to be part of India or part of Pakistan. Evolution of Kashmiri opinion since means that any referendum must allow for a third option: independence. The only international forum that could force a referendum is the UN. It can impose an arms embargo and other sanctions on India and Pakistan if they ignore UN resolutions.

The Rwanda Debacle

The UN missed a similar opportunity to prevent the planet's last act of genocide in Rwanda in 1994. President [Bill] Clinton did not want the UN to intervene. He feared that invoking the UN's Genocide Convention would mean sending

American troops again to Africa in the aftermath of the Somalia debacle. The UN commander in Rwanda, Canadian General Romeo Dallaire, had 2,500 troops. He pleaded with the chief of peacekeeping in New York for another 3,000, plus armoured cars and other protective equipment, to prevent the genocide that his informants assured him was on the way.

His UN force was so ill-prepared that General Dallaire cabled to the UN: 'They [UN troops] will hand over these local people for inevitable killing rather than use their weapons to save local people.' The local UN commander in Kigali, Belgian Colonel Luc Marchal, told me later: 'I still have the feeling that we were in a desert . . . during weeks and weeks, we were crying and nobody answered us.' More than 800,000 Rwandans were butchered by Hutu extremists using rifles, machetes and knives.

The US, Belgium and France were informed about conditions in Rwanda. So was the head of UN peacekeeping, Kofi Annan. Neither Annan nor the US ambassador to the UN, Madeleine Albright, informed the UN or called for an emergency session. Annan became UN Secretary General. Albright was appointed Secretary of State by Bill Clinton, who went on to win a second term of office. The lesson was: keep quiet, ignore genocide and win promotion.

Rwandans killed nearly a million of their own with primitive weapons. How many more can Vajpayee and Musharraf kill with their armouries of mass destruction? What precedent will UN inaction now set for other countries—Russia, China or Israel—considering the quick fix of an atomic bomb or two?

Perhaps times have not changed all that much. On Armistice Day in 1948, American General Omar Bradley lamented: 'Ours is a world of nuclear giants and ethical infants.'

Periodical Bibliography

The following articles have been selected to supplement the diverse views presented in this chapter.

Mohammed Ayoob	"South Asia's Dangers and U.S. Foreign Policy," *Orbis*, Winter 2001.
Benazir Bhutto	"War Is Likely If Musharraf Stays; A Regime Change Is Necessary to Head Off Nuclear Brinkmanship with India," *Los Angeles Times*, May 29, 2002.
Current Events	"On the Brink: Are India and Pakistan Headed for War?" February 1, 2002.
Sumit Ganguly	"Behind India's Bomb: The Politics and Strategy of Nuclear Deterrence," *Foreign Affairs*, September/October 2001.
Peter Grier	"A Big Test of Nuclear Deterrence," *Christian Science Monitor*, January 4, 2002.
Hinduism Today	"Kashmir's Crisis," January–March 2002. www.hinduismtoday.com.
Nisjid Jajari	"Fuzzy Red Lines: Nobody Can Predict If or When the Nukes Might Fly," *Newsweek*, June 3, 2002.
M.V. Ramana and A.H. Nayyar	"India, Pakistan, and the Bomb," *Scientific American*, December 2001.
Jaswant Singh	"Against Nuclear Apartheid," *Foreign Affairs*, September/October 1998.
Strobe Talbott	"Dealing with the Bomb in South Asia," *Foreign Affairs*, March/April 1999.
Achin Vanaik	"False Hope in Deterrence," *Hindustan Times*, May 29, 2002. www.tni.org.
Eric Weiner	"Islamabad Dispatch: Trigger Happy," *New Republic*, June 24, 2002.
Lally Weymouth	"Voices from a Hot Zone," *Newsweek*, July 2, 2002.
Kevin Whitelaw et al.	"Losing Gambit," *U.S. News & World Report*, June 17, 2002.
Fareed Zakaria	"In Praise of Nukes (Gulp)," *Newsweek*, June 10, 2002.

CHAPTER 2

What Is the Status of Human Rights in India and Pakistan?

Chapter Preface

Both India and Pakistan have done something that the United States has never accomplished—each nation has elected a woman as its political leader. Indira Gandhi served as prime minister of India from 1966 to 1977 and again from 1980 to 1984. Benazir Bhutto was Pakistan's prime minister from 1988 to 1990 and again from 1993 to 1996. In addition to these heads of state, women have been elected and appointed to many other government positions in both nations.

However, despite this record and the fact that the constitutions of both nations include provisions banning gender-based discrimination, human rights organizations have criticized the general performance of both nations in protecting women's rights. Women's rights in Pakistan, with its 97 percent Muslim population, have been impeded by tribal and Islamic attitudes and customs. For example, in Pakistan most women are expected to interact with the wider world only through male kinsmen. In addition, many are victimized by domestic abuse, including rape and murder, and often find little recourse through the government and criminal justice system. According to a 2000 newspaper survey cited by the international organization Amnesty International, nine out of ten women in Pakistan are ignorant of their most basic rights.

India is generally viewed as having a better record than its neighbor concerning women's rights. But India's government has also been criticized for failing to protect women from domestic abuse and violence. A 2001 United Nations report concluded that almost two-thirds of Indian women have been subjected to some form of domestic abuse. Thousands of women each year are murdered by their husbands who are upset with the dowries they received from their wives' families. In the 1990s India's government did pass many laws guaranteeing women's rights and strengthening their position in the family and workplace, but long-standing cultural patterns are difficult to change, according to social scientist Partha Chatterjee. "These were among the most progressive laws anywhere," he notes, "but actual practices on the ground have not necessarily changed much."

Women's rights in India and Pakistan are not the only cause

for concern for international human rights organizations. Both nations have been criticized for failing to protect the basic human rights of their people—especially members of religious minorities (non-Muslims in Pakistan, non-Hindus in India). The viewpoints in this chapter provide a sampling of the debates currently being waged over the status of human rights in India and Pakistan.

"The Constitution of India has set a model in matters of minority rights."

India Protects Minority Rights

Asghar Ali Engineer

Asghar Ali Engineer is a civil rights activist and head of two organizations: the Institute of Islamic Studies and the Centre for the Study of Society and Secularism. He has written and edited numerous books on ethnic problems in South Asia. In the following viewpoint, he emphasizes how India is a multi-cultural country with great diversity in its peoples, languages, and religions. In order to protect the rights of its linguistic and religious minorities, India's constitution grants them special rights and guarantees. India may serve as a model for other nations in protecting minority rights, he argues.

As you read, consider the following questions:

1. How is India different from the United States and countries in Europe, according to Engineer?
2. What problems does the author describe in attempting to define "minority"?
3. What has been the fate of Muslims who moved to Pakistan, according to Engineer?

Asghar Ali Engineer, "Minorities: Many-Splendoured Contributions," *Independent India: The First Fifty Years*, edited by Hiranmay Karlekar. Delhi: Oxford University Press, 1998. Copyright © 1998 by the Indian Council for Cultural Relations. Reproduced by permission.

India is a country of bewildering diversity. No single community can claim the entire credit for the richness of its culture and traditions. India has inherited a composite culture both in the North and South, thanks to the contribution of various religious and cultural communities. Despite this diversity India has maintained its unity. Those who led the freedom struggle, always felt proud of this and reiterated its character as 'Unity in Diversity'.

Not a Melting Pot

The classical model of an European nation is mono-religious, mono-lingual and mono-cultural. The very basis of nationhood in Europe was one language and culture. In this sense India is multi-national in character. There is bewildering diversity on every front—linguistic, cultural or religious. And it has been historically so. India has never been a nation in the classical sense. Yet our leaders performed the miracle of carving out a modern nation from a multi-lingual, multi-religious and multi-cultural country. Indians can justly be proud of this. In fact we have made diversity our virtue and strength. In Western countries pluralism has been accepted only in the post-modernist era. The United States of America used to take pride in what it called the 'melting-pot model' of nation building. All those who migrated to North America discarded their original European identity and constructed a new American identity. Thus diversity was considered undesirable and mono-culturalism a great virtue. But this was possible as long as the migrants were mainly from European (Western) civilization. When in the post–Second World War or post-colonial era the migration to USA took place more from Asian and African countries, the melting-pot model had to be replaced by the mosaic model. However, India has for centuries adopted the mosaic model. And it is this which has given its society so much richness and colour. All religious and cultural communities have contributed richly to Indian society. . . .

Defining "Minority"

There is a great deal of controversy about the concept of a minority. Many scholars maintain that in a democracy there could be only a political majority and minorities, not religious ones. These scholars refuse to entertain the concept of religious minorities in a liberal democracy like India.

These scholars may have a point. But this is possible only when we have a perfect liberal democracy; that is, when religion has no role to play in our political or social life. However, that is a distant dream. We cannot conceive of a society in the near future in which religion does not deeply influence social, political and cultural lives. Also, we have our own historical legacy which cannot be wished away. We had major conflicts between Hindus and Muslims on the question of sharing power (i.e. in the political arena) and our country was divided. Thus the communal question has become part of our historical legacy and the concepts of reli-

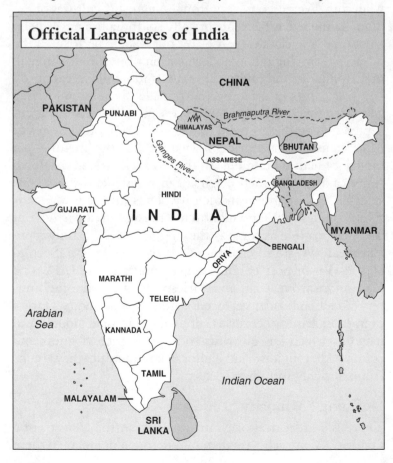

gious minority and majority have their own dynamics.

The framers of our Constitution were well aware of this legacy and hence the concept of religious minorities was accepted in good faith and certain special rights were guaranteed to them in the Constitution in Articles 25 to 30. Article 25 says that 'subject to public order, morality and health and to the other provisions of this part, all persons are equally entitled to freedom of conscience and the right freely to profess, practice and propagate religion'. Similarly Article 26 guarantees freedom to manage religious affairs, and Article 29 takes care of rights of cultural and linguistic minorities. Article 30, on the other hand, gives cultural and linguistic minorities the right to establish their own institutions.

Model for Other Countries

Thus it will be seen that the Constitution of India recognizes both religious as well as cultural and linguistic minorities. In fact the Constitution of India has set a model in matters of minority rights which could be followed by other countries. Even Britain does not have adequate laws to take care of its Hindu, Muslim and Buddhist minorities. British society has yet to come to grips with the problem of its religious minorities. There are quite a few discriminatory laws against which religious minorities, especially the Muslims, are protesting. Now even the United Nations Organisation has accepted the need for a charter of minority rights, which it adopted in December 1992. In the post-colonial period there is no country in the world which does not have one religious minority or another.

Another question concerns the definition of minority. There are different types of minorities apart from religious or linguistic and cultural ones—for example, dominant or dominated minorities. A religious, cultural or linguistic minority can be dominant or dominated. Similarly an economic minority—usually the feudal or capitalist class—dominates a majority and this feudal or capitalist class may be coterminous with a particular religion or culture. The Muslims in pre-British India, for example, were a feudal ruling class. Yet in a religious sense they were a small minority. And this had its own consequences. In fact when a dominant minority becomes a dominated minority it faces serious consequences. And there lies the negative fallout of the communal question. . . .

Composite Culture

One cannot think of any religious community which did not participate in India's freedom struggle. The Indian National Congress, in fact, was an umbrella organization and it threw open its membership to all communities. Right at its inception in 1885, people of all religious communities joined it. In fact its first three presidents came from minority communities: Badruddin Tyabji, a Muslim from Bombay, W.S. Bonerjee, a Christian from Bengal, and Dadabhai Naorojee, a Parsi from Bombay. All these communities made tremendous sacrifices throughout the freedom struggle besides richly contributing to India's emerging democratic political culture. . . .

A Warning About Pakistan

Maulana Azad became the first Education Minister of India. He more than deserved to hold this important portfolio in view of his learning. Though Maulana Azad did not receive modern education in a Western university like many of his colleagues, he . . . had a remarkable breadth of vision and put higher education on a sound footing. He also took steps to encourage scientific and technological research in post-Independence India. . . .

Maulana Azad was totally opposed to the very concept of Pakistan. He staunchly believed in composite nationalism. He told a group of Muslims from Uttar Pradesh who were bound for Pakistan:

> You are leaving your motherland. Do you know what the consequences will be? Your frequent exoduses such as this will weaken the Muslims of India. A time may come when the various Pakistani regions start asserting their separate identities; Bengali, Punjabi, Sindhi, Balochi may declare themselves separate *quoms* [nations]. Will your position in Pakistan at that time be anything better than that of uninvited guests? The Hindu can be your religious opponent but not your regional and national opponent. You can deal with this situation. But in Pakistan, at any time you may have to face regional and national opposition; before this kind of opposition you will be helpless.

And helpless they are today. The Muhajirs (immigrants from Uttar Pradesh and Bihar) today are facing exactly the situation the Maulana predicted. They have become unwanted guests and are at the receiving end. The Maulana could visualize this and had warned the Muslims in time.

However, for the Muslims in India he was quite optimistic. He told the students of Aligarh Muslim University in a convocation address,

> I am not aware what the state of your minds is today, nor in what colours the future appears to you. Does it bring to you the message of closing doors or opening gates that introduce you to new vistas of experience? I do not know what visions are before you, but I will tell you what visions I see. You perhaps feel that doors that were open have been closed. I see that doors that were closed have now opened. . . . What you and I hear are different. You hear the sound of closing doors but I of doors open. . . .

It will thus be seen that Maulana Azad infused a new confidence among the battered Muslims and gave them a new vision and made them feel an integral part of India.

> *"India, for all its pretense to commanding the world's largest democracy, has been pretty churlish to . . . national groups within its boundaries."*

India Oppresses Its Minority Groups

James P. Lucier

In the following viewpoint, James P. Lucier argues that India has a deserved reputation as a country that mistreats both neighboring nations and ethnic and religious minority groups within its borders. Among the groups oppressed by India's Hindu majority are Muslims and Christians throughout India, ethnic Tamils in southern India, Sikhs in India's Punjab province, and the people of Kashmir. Lucier suggests that the ultimate solution to minority mistreatment may lie in the breakup of India into four or five separate countries. He is a contributing editor for *Insight on the News*, a weekly newsmagazine.

As you read, consider the following questions:
1. What paradox does India present, according to Lucier?
2. How many states and languages exist within India, as stated by the author?
3. What price has India paid for its repression of minority groups, according to Lucier?

The word *thug* is a legacy to English from the Hindi language, as well as *thuggee*, defined as the art and science of thuggery. In 19th century India, the Thugs were organized bands of zealots who roamed the countryside taking as much pleasure in taking whatever pleased them as in the mayhem which caused so much distress to their victims.

A Paradox

India presents a paradox. Individual Indians can be charming, brilliant, provocative, intelligent, creative and spiritual in outlook. But, alas, too often their government draws its main characteristics from the strain in history represented by the historical Thugs, both in dealing with their neighbors and with the minority groups within their borders. Indeed, India's failure to deal honestly with its ethnic problems is at the root of the so-called arms race between India and Pakistan. . . .

India has a reputation as a bully. The government of India, for all its pretense to commanding the world's largest democracy, has been pretty churlish to its neighbors, as well as to the national groups within its boundaries. Its irredentism swallowed up Christian Goa to the applause of liberals dancing at the shrine of Mahatma Ghandi. It has twice fought wars with Pakistan, and has been a nuclear power since 1974. It fomented the horribly bloody breakup of East Pakistan, now Bangladesh, and has continued attempts to subvert Bangladesh's independence. It has engaged in border wars against China over disputed territory, and it boldly took over Sikkim and made it an Indian state. It has refused to give the citizens of Kashmir a fair shake on voting for independence, despite resolutions of the U.N. Security Council. It has designs on the part of Kashmir that was assigned to Pakistan by the agreements of 1947.

Christians throughout the whole region routinely are harassed, even murdered, while Indian officials look the other way, and the Tamils in the south are the object of special persecution. India meanwhile has conducted ruthless repression against the Sikhs in Punjab, keeping that territory under a bitter martial law that has a long history of official murder, torture and disappearance of its enemies. Indeed, it leveled even the Sikhs' famous Golden Temple, the Akal Takh, in

Amritsar, containing the sacred sanctuary and library of the Sikh religion, on the pretext that some rebels holed up there posed a threat to India. It is as though Mussolini had blown up St. Peter's Basilica and burnt the Vatican library on the grounds that the Swiss Guards were an obstacle to the security of fascism.

Hindus and Muslims

India is 80 percent Hindu, but if the number of Muslims in India were counted as one country, it would be the second-largest Muslim country in the world. Yet the followers of Islam have learned to keep a low profile. The crowd that now is in control in New Delhi is the same one that incited Hindu mobs in 1992 to tear down, brick by brick, the Babri Mesjid, a 16th century mosque built by the Mogul emperors in Ayodhya. The same Hindu nationalism incited the ruling Bharatiya Janata Party, or BJP, to inflame tensions by conducting unneeded nuclear tests in 1998. Nice people, these Thugs.

There are 27 states (including the Delhi region), with a vast assemblage of peoples speaking more than 50 main languages. Ironically, only the English language binds them together.

India knows that the state of Jammu and Kashmir is majority Muslim, and that if a referendum ever were held, as required by U.N. Security Council resolutions, it immediately would choose to join with Pakistan. India knows that in Punjab the majority is Sikh and the majority of Sikhs would want to resurrect the late 18th century empire of Sarkar-e-Khalsa as a nation called Khalistan. India knows that Assam also has a flourishing separatist movement. All three states have suffered under a brutalizing form of martial law.

Failure to meet ethnic and religious aspirations head-on repeatedly have made India a scene of tragedy. The wars with Pakistan, the brutal repressions and the incitement of sectarian violence have brought a terrible backlash for which India already has paid much too heavy a price: the assassinations of Prime Minister Indira Ghandi [in 1984] by her Sikh bodyguards and of Rajiv Ghandi [in 1991] by Tamil separatists. The truth is that India really is four or five nations which will not be at rest with one another until a peaceful devolution takes place in the manner of the former Soviet Union.

"Church leaders . . . have pleaded in vain for the government to curtail the violence of Hindu mobs against Christians."

Christians Are Mistreated in India

Jeff M. Sellers

More than 80 percent of India's people are Hindus, but the nation's population also includes more than 100 million Muslims (12.5 percent of the population) and 22 million Christians (2.5 percent). In the following viewpoint, Jeff M. Sellers argues that despite guarantees of religious freedom written in India's constitution, Christians in India have been victims of both violent attacks and local laws that restrict their activities. Sellers blames Hindu extremists who call Christianity a dangerous "foreign religion" for the mistreatment Christians receive in India. He also criticizes the Indian government for failing to protect Christians. Sellers is an associate editor for *Christianity Today* magazine.

As you read, consider the following questions:
1. What examples of violence against Christians does Sellers describe?
2. What role does India's ruling BJP political party have regarding mistreatment of Christians, according to the author?
3. What motivates Hindus who attack Christians, according to Sellers?

Jeff M. Sellers, "Hounded, Beaten, Shot," *Christianity Today*, vol. 46, June 10, 2002, p. 48. Copyright © 2002 by Jeff M. Sellers. Reproduced by permission.

L ast August 27, 2001, Hindu militants in the village of Mehndikheda, Madhya Pradesh state, chased Christians from a Pentecostal prayer service and destroyed their meeting place. Two weeks later, near Calcutta, Hindu extremists burned Christian books they had seized from schoolchildren. A week later in Gujarat state, Hindus severely beat Methodist pastor Paul Christian and four of his church members for showing a film about Jesus.

Hindu Radicalism

Such incidents have become more common since the Hindu nationalist Bharatiya Janata Party (BJP) and its allies came to power in 1998. For half a century the government has given religious minorities a role in Indian society, but now the BJP condones radical Hindu elements that forcibly strive to turn the world's largest democracy into a Hindu-only nation.

The radicals' fusion of Hinduism with nationalism—Hindutva—has struck primarily at Muslims, but violence against Christians also has surged in 2002. Attacks on Christians occur weekly, *The Washington Times* noted on February 25, 2002. In one case, militants shot two church workers and a teenage boy; in another, extremists beat two missionaries as they were bicycling home; and a mob of 70 Hindus attacked a group of children attending a catechism class in a church.

India has known various religions throughout its history, but extremists of the National Volunteer Movement (RSS, the Rashtriya Swayamsevak Sangh) advocate a return to ancient days of Hindu glory described in scriptures such as the Bhagavad-Gita. Eighty percent of India's population adhere to some form of Hinduism, 12.5 percent are Muslim, and 2.4 percent are Christian, according to [the book] *Operation World*.

Attacks on Christianity

India's constitution calls for full religious freedom. But nationalists, portraying Christianity as a "foreign religion," have succeeded in passing local legislation that limits Christian activities and conversions in some states. In November 1999, Orissa state—where Hindu extremists killed missionary Graham Staines and his two sons in 1999—passed an or-

Violence Against Christians

The formation in March 1998 of Prime Minister Atal Behari Vajpayee's Bharatiya Janata Party government was followed by violence against Christians in more than half of India's 25 states, concentrated largely in the north and west where Christians are few and Hindu nationalism is particularly strong. One of the most notorious incidents occurred in the central Indian state of Madhya Pradesh. At about 2 A.M. on Sept. 23, four nuns who operate a medical clinic in the state were dragged from their convent and gang-raped by a dozen or more men. This shocking crime set off huge protests across the country, but the World Hindu Federation, an organization with ties to the ruling B.J.P., virtually justified the attacks, claiming they resulted from "the anger of patriotic Hindu youth against the anti-national forces."

The following months witnessed an outbreak of violent actions by Hindu mobs against Christians such as had not been seen before. The *Times of India* noted that, having long targeted the Muslims and the Sikhs, Hindu extremists were now turning to the small and unprotected minority of Indian Christians. Nowhere was this more evident than in the northwestern state of Gujarat.

Although it is the birthplace and served as the base of Mohandas K. Gandhi, father of the nation and model of religious tolerance, Gujarat has witnessed the largest number of anti-Christian attacks, some 60 recorded incidents in just the second half of 1998, between June and Christmas Day, and an almost equal number of anti-Christian incidents in the few weeks after Christmas. Most of the attacks have been against church property—schools, health centers, chapels—but houses and shops of Christians have also been ransacked and looted, and Bibles have been burned and individuals beaten.

Thomas Quigley, *America*, April 3, 1999.

---

der prohibiting religious conversions without the prior permission of local police and district magistrates.

Additionally, 1.2 million schoolchildren are now learning a false version of history that disparages Christianity, according to Zenit News Agency. The national government relies on the support of the RSS and the militant World Hindu Council (VHP, the Vishna Hindu Parishad) and has provided them political patronage. This has enabled the extremists—whose Hindutva ideology asserts that "India is Hindu only"—to rewrite the nation's history.

Church leaders in India have pleaded in vain for the government to curtail the violence of Hindu mobs against Christians. In March 2002, RSS activists attacked two Catholic priests on their way to a police station to report an attack on a church-run school in Khurda, according to the SAR news agency. The previous day, RSS and VHP extremists pillaged and set fire to a mission station of the Divine Word Society in Sanjeli, Gujarat.

Government Inaction

Prime Minister Atal Behari Vajpayee has failed to take strong action against rampant Hindu extremism, rights organizations say. He has held up some Hindu fanatics as exemplary. . . .

The U.S. Commission on International Religious Freedom has recommended that the [U.S. government] . . . more swiftly and explicitly urge the BJP to condemn and halt the violence against religious minorities.

*"If ever there was persecution, it was of the
Hindus at the hands of Christians."*

Christians Are Not Mistreated in India

Francois Gautier

Francois Gautier, a French-born journalist based in India, is
the correspondent for the French newspaper *Le Figaro* and
the author of *Rewriting Indian History*. In the following viewpoint, he presents his views on how Christians are treated in
India. Allegations of Christian "persecution," he contends,
are based on factual errors in reports and a shallow appreciation of Indian history. In fact, during India's history, Christians often persecuted Hindus and fraudulently or forcibly
converted them to Christianity. He concludes by asserting
that Hinduism is a religion of tolerance and that Indians
must take steps to protect their religion and their culture.

As you read, consider the following questions:
1. What historical examples of Christian persecution does
   Gautier describe?
2. What lies behind many recent stories of violence against
   Christians, according to the author?
3. What opinions does Gautier express on the subject of
   religious conversion?

When Prime Minister Vajpayee was in the US in September 2000, the National Association of Asian Christians (NAAIC) in the US (whom nobody had heard about before), paid 50,000 dollars to the *New York Times* to publish 'an Open Letter to the Hon'ble Atal Bihari Vajpayee, prime minister of India'.

While 'warmly welcoming the PM', the NAAIC expressed deep concern about the 'persecution' of Christians in India by 'extremist' (meaning Hindu) groups, mentioning as examples 'the priest, missionaries and church workers who have been murdered', the nuns 'raped', and the potential enacting of conversion laws, which would make 'genuine' conversions illegal. The letter concluded by saying 'that Christians in India today live in fear'.

The whole affair was an embarrassment (as it was intended to be) to Mr Vajpayee and the Indian delegation, which had come to prod American businessmen to invest in India, a peaceful, pro-Western and democratic country.

I am born a Christian and I have had a strong Catholic education. I do believe that Christ was an incarnation of Pure Love and that His Presence still radiates in the world. I also believe there are human beings who sincerely try to incarnate the ideals of Jesus and that you can find today in India a few missionaries (such as Father Ceyrac, a French Jesuit, who works mostly with lepers in Tamil Nadu), who are incarnations of that Love, tending tirelessly to people, without trying to convert them.

But I have also lived for more than 30 years in India, I am married to an Indian, I have traveled the length and breath of this country and I have evolved a love and an understanding of India, which few other foreign correspondents have, because they are never posted long enough to start getting a real feeling of this vast and often baffling country (nobody can claim to fully understand India). And this is what I have to say about the 'persecution' of Christians in India.

A Brief History

Firstly, it is necessary to bring about a little bit of a historical flashback, which very few foreign correspondents (and unfortunately also Indian journalists) care to do, which would make for a more balanced view of the problem.

If ever there was persecution, it was of the Hindus at the hands of Christians, who were actually welcomed in this country, as they have been welcomed in no other place on this planet. Indeed, the first Christian community of the world, that of the Syrian Christians, was established in Kerala in the first century; they were able to live in peace and practice their religion freely, even imbibing some of the local Hindu customs, until the Jesuits came in the 16th century and told them it was 'heathen' to have anything to do with the Hindus, thereby breaking the Syrian Church in two.

When [Portuguese explorer] Vasco de Gama landed in Kerala in 1498, he was generously received by the Zamorin, the Hindu king of Calicut, who granted him the right to establish warehouses for commerce. But once again, Hindu tolerance was exploited and the Portuguese wanted more and more. In 1510, [Portuguese colonizer] Alfonso de Albuquerque seized [the territory of] Goa, where he started a reign of terror, burning 'heretics', crucifying Brahmins, using false theories to forcibly convert the lower castes, razing temples to build churches upon them and encouraging his soldiers to take Indian mistresses.

Indeed, the Portuguese perpetrated here some of the worst atrocities ever committed in Asia by Christianity upon another religion. Ultimately, the Portuguese had to be kicked out of India [in 1961], when all other colonisers had already left.

Christianity and British Rule

British missionaries in India were always supporters of colonialism; they encouraged it and their whole structure was based on 'the good Western civilised world being brought to the Pagans'. Because, in the words of Claudius Bucchanan, a chaplain attached to the East India Company, 'Neither truth, nor honesty, honour, gratitude, nor charity, is to be found in the breast of a Hindoo'! What a comment about a nation that gave the world the Vedas [Hindu sacred texts] at a time when Europeans were still grappling in their caves!

And it is in this way that the British allowed entire chunks of territories in the East, where lived tribals [indigenous peoples who customarily lived on the margins of Indian society], whose poverty and simplicity made them easy prey, to be converted to Christianity. By doing so, the Christian missionaries cut a people from their roots and tradition, made them look westwards towards a culture and a way of life which was not theirs.

And the result is there today for everyone to see: it is in these eastern states, some of which are 90 per cent Christian, that one finds the biggest drug problems (and crime) in India. It should also be said that many of the eastern separatist movements have been covertly encouraged by Christian missionaries on the ground that 'tribals were there before the "Aryan Hindus" invaded India and imposed Hinduism upon them'.

Western Bias

Western understanding of religious persecution in India, fed largely by exaggerated and biased media reports, is woefully distorted. This lack of understanding becomes even more troubling in light of efforts by Christian missionaries in India to gain an international forum for a solution to their problems. By turning to Western countries for support, Indian Christians may be undermining their own interests. Misapplied policies from the West, based on inadequate information, could actually work to alienate Christians from their own society.

Vatsala Vedantam, *Christian Century*, April 14, 1999.

The trouble is that the latest archaeological and linguistic discoveries point out to the fact that there NEVER was an Aryan invasion of India—it just was an invention of the British and the missionaries to serve their purpose.

Secondly, Christianity has always striven on the myth of persecution, which in turn bred 'martyrs' and saints, indispensable to the propagation of Christianity. But it is little known, for instance, that the first 'saints' of Christianity, 'martyred' in Rome, a highly refined civilisation, which had evolved a remarkable system of gods and goddesses, some of whom were derived from Hindu mythology via the Greeks, were actually killed (a normal practice in those days), while bullying peaceful Romans to embrace the 'true' religion, in the same way that later Christian missionaries will browbeat 'heathen' Hindus, adoring many gods, into believing that Jesus was the only 'true' god.

Investigating Recent Cases

Now to come to the recent cases of persecution of Christians in India at the hands of Hindu groups. I have personally investigated quite a few, amongst them the rape of the four nuns in Jhabua, MP, nearly two years ago [in 1998]. This rape is still quoted as an example of the 'atrocities' committed by Hindus on Christians.

Yet, when I interviewed the four innocent nuns, they themselves admitted, along with George Anatil, the bishop of Indore, that it had nothing to do with religion: it was the doing of a gang of Bhil tribals, known to perpetrate this kind of hateful acts on their own women. Today, the Indian press, the Christian hierarchy and the politicians, continue to include the Jhabua rape in the list of atrocities against the Christians.

Or take the burning of churches in Andhra Pradesh a few months ago [June 8, 2000], which was supposed to have been committed by the 'fanatic' RSS [Rashtriya Swayamsevak Sangh, a controversial organization that advocates Hindu nationalism]. It was proved later that it was actually the handiwork of Indian Muslims, at the behest of the ISI [Pakistan's Inter-Services Intelligence agency] to foment hatred between Christians and Hindus. Yet the Indian press which went berserk at the time of the burnings, mostly kept quiet when the true nature of the perpetrators was revealed.

Finally, even if Dara Singh does belong to the Bajrang Dal, it is doubtful if the hundred other accused do.[1] What is more probable, is that like in many other 'backward' places, it is a case of converted tribals versus non-converted tribals, of pent-up jealousies, of old village feuds and land disputes. It is also an outcome of what—it should be said—are the ag-

1. Dara Singh was the accused leader of a mob that on January 22, 1999, killed Australian missionary Graham Staines and his two sons by burning them alive in their vehicle. The Bajrang Dal is a militant organization of Hindu extremists.

gressive methods of the Pentecost and Seventh Adventists missionaries, known for their muscular ways of conversion.

Fraudulent Conversions

Thirdly, conversions in India by Christian missionaries of low caste Hindus and tribals are sometimes nothing short of fraudulent and shameful. American missionaries are investing huge amounts of money in India, which come from donation drives in the United States where gullible Americans think the dollars they are giving go towards uplifting 'poor and uneducated Indians'.

It is common in Kerala, for instance, particularly in the poor coastal districts, to have 'miracle boxes' put in local churches: the gullible villager writes out a paper mentioning his wish: a fishing boat, a loan for a pucca [permanent] house, fees for the son's schooling. . . . And lo, a few weeks later, the miracle happens! And of course the whole family converts, making others in the village follow suit.

American missionaries (and their government) would like us to believe that democracy includes the freedom to convert by any means. But France for example, a traditionally Christian country, has a minister who is in charge of hunting down 'sects'. And by sects, it is meant anything that does not fall within the recognised family of Christianity—even the Church of Scientology, favoured by some Hollywood stars such as Tom Cruise or John Travolta, is ruthlessly hounded. And look at . . . how innocent children and women were burnt down by the FBI (with the assistance of the US army) at Waco, Texas, because they belonged to a dangerous sect . . .

Did you know that Christianity is dying in the West? Not only is church attendance falling dramatically because spirituality has deserted it, but less and less youth find the vocation to become priests or nuns. And as a result, say in the rural parts of France, you will find only one priest for six or seven villages, whereas till the late seventies, the smallest hamlet had its own parish priest.

And where is Christianity finding new priests today? In the Third World, of course! And India, because of the innate impulsion of its people towards god, is a very fertile recruiting ground for the Church, particularly in Kerala and Tamil

Nadu. Hence the huge attention that India is getting from the United States, Australia, or England and the massive conversion drive going on today.

It is sad that Indians, once converted, specially the priests and nuns, tend to turn against their own country and help in the conversion drive. There are very few 'White' missionaries left in India and most of the conversions are done today by Indian priests.

In September 2000, during the bishops's conference in Bangalore, it was restated by bishops and priests from all over India that conversion is the FIRST priority of the Church here. But are the priests and bishops aware that they would never find in any Western country the same freedom to convert that they take for granted in India? Do they know that in China they would be expelled, if not put into jail? Do they realise that they have been honoured guests in this country for nearly two thousand years and that they are betraying those that gave them peace and freedom?

Hinduism: The Religion of Tolerance

Hinduism, the religion of tolerance, the coming spirituality of this new millennium, has survived the unspeakable barbarism of wave after wave of Muslim invasions, the insidious onslaught of Western colonialism which has killed the spirit of so many Third World countries and the soul-stifling assault of Nehruvianism.[2] But will it survive the present Christian offensive?

Many Hindu religious leaders feel Christianity is a real threat today, as in numerous ways it is similar to Hinduism, from which Christ borrowed so many concepts (see Sri Siri Ravi Shankar's book: *Hinduism and Christianity*).

It is thus necessary that Indians themselves become more aware of the danger their culture and unique civilisation is facing at the hands of missionaries sponsored by foreign money. It is also necessary that they stop listening to the Marxist-influenced English newspapers's defence of the right of Christian missionaries to convert innocent Hindus.

2. Jawaharlal Nehru, India's prime minister from 1947 to 1964, has been criticized by some Hindus for promoting a secular rather than a Hindu government for India.

Conversion belongs to the times of colonialism. We have entered in the era of Unity, of coming together, of tolerance and accepting each other as we are—not of converting in the name of one elusive 'true' god.

When Christianity accepts the right of other people to follow their own beliefs and creeds, then only will Jesus Christ's spirit truly radiate in the world.

"The . . . suppression by India is clearly designed to silence the people of Jammu and Kashmir through sheer brutality."

India Has Mistreated the Kashmiri People

Pakistan Ministry of Foreign Affairs

The state of Jammu and Kashmir (often called simply Kashmir), located in the highlands between India and Pakistan, was claimed by both nations when they became independent of Great Britain in 1947. A 1947–1948 war left Kashmir divided along a so-called Line of Control between India and Pakistan—a division that remains to this day. In the following viewpoint, the Pakistan Ministry of Foreign Affairs presents its version of Kashmir's history since 1947. It argues that the people of Kashmir (the majority of whom are Muslim) wanted to join Pakistan in 1947, but were prevented from doing so by the Indian government. India prevented a vote by Kashmir's people, called for by the United Nations, from ever taking place. The Pakistan ministry asserts that after decades of suffering mistreatment by India, the Kashmiri people began an indigenous struggle against Indian occupation—a struggle India has met with brute force. It concludes by pledging its support for a peaceful settlement that would allow Kashmir's people to decide their fate.

As you read, consider the following questions:

1. What promises did Indian leaders make on the eve of independence regarding Kashmir, according to the Pakistan Ministry of Foreign Affairs?
2. What human rights violations do the authors describe?

Pakistan Ministry of Foreign Affairs, "Jammu & Kashmir Dispute," www.forisb.org.

This dispute dates back to the partition of the British Indian Empire, in August 1947, into two independent states, Pakistan and India. At that time there were also around 565 princely states, large and small, which were under British suzerainty but were not directly ruled by the British Government. Most of these states joined either India or Pakistan taking into account their contiguity to one or the other country and the wishes of their people.

There were, however, some states over which problems arose, primarily because of India's insatiable desire to grab territory. For example, the Muslim ruler of Junagarh, a state with a Hindu majority population, announced his decision to join Pakistan. India responded by aiding and abetting the establishment of a so-called "Provisional Government" of Junagarh on Indian territory, which attacked Junagarh with Indian connivance and support. Subsequently Indian forces also invaded Junagarh, despite protests from Pakistan, in order to "restore law and order". A farcical plebiscite was organized under Indian auspices, and India annexed Junagarh. Similarly, in Hyderabad, a Hindu majority state, the Muslim ruler of the state wanted to retain an independent status. India responded by attacking Hyderabad and annexed the state by force. India sought to justify its aggression against Hyderabad and Junagarh on the plea that the rulers of Junagarh and Hyderabad were acting against the wishes of their people.

In Jammu and Kashmir state, the situation was the reverse. The ruler of the State was a Hindu, while the population was overwhelmingly Muslim and wanted to join Pakistan. In this case, India consistently pressurized the Hindu Ruler to accede to India. Apprehending that the Hindu ruler was likely to succumb to Indian pressure, the people of Jammu and Kashmir rose against him, forcing him to flee from Srinagar, the capital of the State. They formed their own government on 24th October, 1947. On 27th of October, 1947, the Government of India alleged that the ruler had acceded to India on the basis of a fraudulent instrument of accession, sent its forces into the State and occupied a large part of Jammu and Kashmir.

But Indian leaders, including Jawaharlal Nehru, the Prime Minister and Lord Mountbatten, the then Governor

General of India, solemnly declared that the final status of Jammu and Kashmir would be decided by the people of the State. This declaration was reiterated by India at the UN Security Council when the dispute was referred to that august body, under chapter 6 of the UN Charter relating to peaceful settlement of disputes. The Security Council adopted a number of resolutions on the issue, providing for the holding of a fair and impartial plebiscite in Jammu and Kashmir under UN auspices to enable the Kashmiri people to exercise their right of self-determination and join either Pakistan or India. The UN also deployed the United Nations Military Observer Group [in India and Pakistan] (UNMOGIP) to monitor the cease-fire line between the Liberated or Azad Kashmir area and the Indian Held Kashmir (IHK). These resolutions were accepted by India and Pakistan and constitute an agreed legal basis for settlement of the dispute.

India, however, thwarted all attempts by the United Nations to organize a plebiscite in the State of Jammu and Kashmir. Eventually, India openly resiled from its commitments and declared that Jammu and Kashmir was an integral part of India.

The Indian armed intervention in the State of Jammu and Kashmir was illegal and took place against the wishes of the Kashmiri people. Despite the decision of the UN Security Council for the holding of a plebiscite to allow the people of Jammu and Kashmir to determine their own future, India's own pledges to that effect, and reiteration of their commitment of resolving the Kashmir issue in the Simla Agreement of 1972 signed between Pakistan and India after the 1971 war, India continues to remain in illegal occupation of a large part of Jammu and Kashmir, refuses to allow the Kashmiris to decide their own future and continues its brutal suppression in the territory. . . .

The Kashmiri People Rise Up

After more than four decades of a peaceful struggle against Indian repression, manipulation and exploitation, the Kashmiri people, convinced that India would never honour its commitments, and inspired by similar movements for freedom in other parts of the world, rose against the Indian occupation towards the later part of 1989. Their struggle was, and remains, largely peaceful. India sought to suppress their movement with massive use of force, killing hundreds of innocent men, women and children. This led some of the Kashmiri youth to take up arms in self defence. Since 1989, more than 60,000 Kashmiri people have been killed in a reign of terror and repression unleashed by over 600,000 Indian troops. Many more languish in Indian jails where they are subjected to torture and custodial deaths. There have been numerous cases of gang rapes of Kashmiri women by the Indian forces and the deliberate burning down of entire localities and villages.

These brutalities have been documented by International and even Indian Human Rights Organizations. Organizations such as Amnesty International and Human Rights Watch as well as Indian human rights non-government organizations (NGOs) have extensively documented the gross and systematic violation of human rights of the Kashmiri people by Indian military and para-military forces. Extra judicial killings, involuntary disappearances, arbitrary detentions, rapes and torture continue to be reported on a large scale. The Kashmiri leaders have been repeatedly harassed and physically intimidated. They have also been denied travel permission to prevent them from exposing Indian human rights abuses in Occupied Jammu and Kashmir. The massive suppression by India is clearly designed to silence the people of Jammu and Kashmir through sheer brutality bordering on genocide and ethnic cleansing.

India refuses to acknowledge that the people of Indian Held Kashmir (IHK) have become totally alienated and there is complete rejection of Indian occupation. Several Kashmiri political parties have formed the All Pakistan Hurriyat (Freedom) Conference (APHC) to continue the political struggle for self-determination. The APHC, therefore, constitutes the true representative of the Kashmiri people.

Blaming Pakistan

Instead of accepting the existing reality, India has sought to blame Pakistan for allegedly promoting the Kashmiri uprising. The fact is that this movement is completely indigenous and enjoys mass support. The Indian allegations against Pakistan are a ploy to mislead the International Community and to create a smokescreen behind which they can continue repression in IHK. Pakistan has offered to enable the UNMOGIP or any other neutral force to monitor the LoC [Line of Control] along which India has deployed several thousands of its troops and has mined the entire area. Indian refusal to accept these proposals exposes their false allegations.

Handelsman. © 2002 by *Newsday*. Reprinted with permission.

A peaceful, negotiated settlement of the Kashmir dispute in accordance with UN resolutions remains on top of Pakistan's foreign policy agenda. To demonstrate its sincerity in finding a peaceful solution to this core issue, Pakistan has always sought a meaningful and substantive dialogue with India. However, the Indians have refused to engage in meaningful talks on Kashmir, claiming the territory as an integral part of India. Only when compelled by extraneous factors or international pressure, such as in 1962–63, 1990–94 and again after May 1998, have the Indians agreed to talks on Kashmir. But this dialogue has been sterile because the Indian objective has never been to find a settlement but to deflect international pressure by creating the facade of talks.

During 1962–63, the Indians agreed to talks on Kashmir under U.S. persuasion at a time when their relations with China had deteriorated and the Sino-Indian war took place and it was necessary for India to protect its western flank with Pakistan. Between 1990–94, India was hard pressed for a dialogue, again due to international pressure following the indigenous Kashmiri uprising which began in the end of 1989. Under pressure from the US, following the mission of the American President's Special envoy, Robert Gates to the region, India engaged in seven rounds of talks at the Foreign Secretary level. Due to continued Indian intransigence, however, this process broke down in January 1994. After a hiatus of three years, talks were resumed at the initiative of Pakistan's former Prime Minister Nawaz Sharif, after he assumed office in March 1997. Following Foreign Secretary level talks in June 1997, an agreed agenda was adopted which includes the specific issue of Kashmir. More importantly, in the meeting between Prime Ministers of Pakistan and India in September 1998, the two leaders agreed that resolution of the Kashmir dispute is essential for peace and security in the region. During Indian Prime Minister [Atal Behari] Vajpayee's visit to Lahore in February 1999, the Lahore Declaration was adopted committing both sides to intensify efforts to resolve the Kashmir issue.

Indian willingness to hold specific talks on Kashmir has been compelled by growing international concern over the Kashmir issue following the nuclear tests by India and in response by Pakistan in May 1998. This nuclearization of South Asia has converted Kashmir into a nuclear flash point and the U.N. Security Council through resolution 1172 as well as . . . a number of world leaders have expressed the urgent need for a dialogue to resolve this root cause of tensions between Pakistan and India.

While the first round of talks on Kashmir was held in October 1998 between the Foreign Secretaries, as per the agreed agenda of June 1997, there was no change in the Indian position. India rejected Pakistan's framework proposal for a structured and substantive dialogue on Kashmir, maintaining its intransigent position that the status of Kashmir was not open for discussion.

Even though India agreed in the Lahore Declaration to intensify efforts to resolve the Kashmir issue, in February 1999, it resorted to delaying tactics for holding the next round of talks. In May 1999, India dealt a severe blow to the dialogue process by launching massive military operations, involving air and ground forces, on the Kashmiri Mujahideen in the Kargil Sector and across the Line of Control on Pakistani controlled areas. The Indians also rejected our efforts to defuse the situation, including the proposal for immediate cessation of hostilities, mutual respect for the LoC and resumption of the dialogue process in accordance with the Lahore Declaration.

At the invitation of President Bill Clinton, former Prime Minister Nawaz Sharif visited the US on 4–5 July 1999 and held indepth discussions with the US President on all aspects of the Kashmir situation. A Joint Statement issued as a result of these talks reflects identity of views on the need to resolve the current situation as well as the larger issue of Kashmir which is central to durable peace and stability in South Asia. It recognizes and underscores the need for both India and Pakistan to respect the LoC in accordance with the 1972 Simla Agreement. It also speaks about concrete steps to be taken for restoration of the LoC. As Pakistan has no presence across the LoC the only concrete step on our part can be to appeal to the Mujahideen who have already achieved their objective of bringing the Kashmir issue back to the international focus of attention.

The two leaders agreed that the Lahore process provides the best forum for resolving all outstanding issues between Pakistan and India including Kashmir. According to the Joint Statement the President of the United States stands committed to his personal involvement to expedite and intensify the process for resolving the Kashmir dispute. This is for the first time that the US has agreed to play a direct role in the search for a final settlement of the Kashmir dispute. India continues to rely on brute force to silence the Kashmiri people. Not only has the campaign of repression been intensified in Indian Occupied Jammu and Kashmir, but additional forces were inducted in November 1998 as part of the new "pro-active" policy and later in the Kargil operation, Indian forces have now been increased to over 730,000. This clearly points to the failure of the current Indian policy to hold the Kashmiri people against their wishes by force.

Pakistan's Position

Pakistani public opinion remains deeply incensed with the wide-spread atrocities committed against the innocent Kashmiri people by Indian military and para-military forces. The government's policy on the Jammu and Kashmir issue enjoys national consensus. Pakistan maintains its principled stand in accordance with the relevant UN Security Council resolutions that call for a plebiscite under UN auspices. It is in keeping with the solemn pledge made to the Kashmiri people by Pakistan, India and the international community.

In order to find an early and just solution to the 50-year old Jammu and Kashmir dispute, Pakistan has welcomed offers of good offices and third-party mediation. It has encouraged the international community to play an active role and facilitate the peaceful settlement of disputes between Pakistan and India.

While Pakistan is committed to a peaceful settlement of the Jammu and Kashmir dispute, adequate measures have been taken to safeguard the country's territorial integrity and national sovereignty.

Pakistan will continue to extend full political, diplomatic and moral support to the legitimate Kashmiri struggle for their right to self-determination as enshrined in the relevant United Nations resolutions. In the context of the bilateral dialogue, it calls on India to translate its commitments into reality. At the same time, it will encourage the international community to support and supplement our efforts to establish lasting peace and stability in South Asia on the basis of equitable resolution of all disputes between the two countries, in particular the core issue of Jammu and Kashmir.

We hope that India will join us in our efforts to bring durable peace to the region for the common benefit of all our peoples. For half a century our region has remained mired in tensions and conflicts. It is our sincere desire to see South Asia enter the next millennium at peace with itself.

*"Pakistan . . . invaded Kashmir against the
will of the people of Kashmir."*

Pakistan Has Mistreated the Kashmiri People

The Statesman

The following viewpoint on Kashmir, a state of India that is
also claimed by Pakistan, is taken from an editorial in *The
Statesman*, one of India's oldest English-language newspapers. The editors address what they view as "myths" about
Kashmir, among which are that Kashmir is under illegiti-
mate Indian occupation. They argue that India has legitimate title to Kashmir due to the fact that its local ruler decided to join India in 1947, and that it is actually Pakistan
that has illegally invaded and occupied parts of Kashmir. In
addition, since 1988 Pakistan has supported and permitted
terrorist groups and individuals to cross over into the Indian
portions of Kashmir, leading to widespread violence and
misery in the region. The editors criticize what they view as
bias in the international media against India.

As you read, consider the following questions:
1. What "myths" about Kashmir have been told by the
   Western media, according to the authors?
2. How does international law support India's claim to
   Pakistan, in the authors' view?
3. What proposals do the editors of *The Statesman* make to
   bring peace to Kashmir?

Facts about Kashmir are mixed with mists and clouds. The western media are portraying Kashmir as the most dangerous place on earth. They have little knowledge about the reality and the history yet they continue to distort facts. The Indian media has so far failed to educate the people, thereby strengthening myths propagated by the western media. These myths are: India had invaded Kashmir in 1948; India had refused to obey the UN Resolutions on Kashmir to hold to the plebiscite to give the opportunity to the people of Kashmir to have their right of self-determination, the violence in Kashmir is mainly homegrown and cannot be solved unless India would give freedom to Kashmir.

Princely State

No matter what the Indian government says, the media outside India has never accepted the Indian story. The recent support of the United States towards India is not reflected in the western media, which still consider India as the guilty party in Kashmir. That is the reason why it is necessary to examine the facts regarding Kashmir.

The Kashmir valley is part of the old princely state of the Jammu and Kashmir (J&K), ruled by the Maharaja until 26 October 1947. Currently the state of J&K is divided among three countries, India has 45 per cent, Pakistan has 35 per cent and China has 20 per cent. The population of the Indian part of Kashmir is about nine million, six million are Muslims, the rest are mainly Hindu and Buddhists. In the Indian part there are three distinct parts with different political and religious features. The Kashmir valley, after the forcible expulsion of Hindus in 1992, is almost 96 per cent Muslim, Jammu is 66 per cent Hindu, and Ladakh is 54 per cent Buddhist. However these facts are unknown to the western media who quite often say that two-thirds of the Kashmir is in India, Pakistan has one third, which is not the case.

Let us take up the issue of "Indian invasion and occupation of Kashmir", as portrayed in the western media and in western academic circles. At the time of the creation of independent India and Pakistan in August 1947, the state of J&K had a "stand-still" agreement with both governments to allow the Maharaja to make up his mind. However, the state of Jammu and Kashmir was invaded by the Pakistan army and Pathan tribesmen on 20 October 1947. Lord Mountbatten, the British Governor-General of India, on 26 October 1947 sent the Indian army headed by a British officer, when the Maharaja of the state of J&K had agreed to join India. The Indian army had the order not to attack the Pakistani position but only to defend; as a result, Pakistan has occupied a substantial part of the Kashmir valley. It has also occupied four small semi-independent kingdoms, part of the state of the J&K, Baltistan, Skardhu, Gilgit and Hunza, where very few Muslims used to live in 1947. These areas are now absorbed into Pakistan as The Northern Area Province.

Accession

Pakistan denies that there was any agreement by which the Maharaja has agreed to join India. The western media ignore this altogether as academic, but it is a legal document whose merit was accepted by the United Nations to whom India made a petition on 30 October 1947 to settle this matter. The government of the United States has accepted legality of the accession. Mr Warren Austin, then the US permanent representative to the United Nations, said, on 4 February 1948 in the Security Council, "The external sovereignty of Kashmir is no longer under the control of the Maharajah . . . with the accession of Jammu and Kashmir to India this foreign sovereignty went over to India and that is why India happens to be here (security council) as a petitioner."

According to international law, if the agreement does not exist or is invalid, as Pakistan argues, then the state of J&K still belongs to the rightful owner, Dr Karan Singh, the son of the Maharaja and therefore the inheritor of the state of J&K. If the agreement exists and is legally valid, then Pakistan or China cannot occupy any parts of the state of J&K. Either way Pakistan cannot win. So they put forward another argument, that the right of the self-determination of the people, not any feudal ownership, should be the supreme.

The [1948] UN Resolution categorically says Pakistan has to withdraw all its troops from areas it had occupied in Kashmir. After Pakistan troops withdrawal, India has to withdraw the bulk of its forces but has to maintain a requisite strength for safeguarding the law and order in the state. Subsequently, the future status of the state was to be determined in accordance with the will of the people. Pakistan never vacated the areas it had occupied, so no plebiscite could take place.

Pakistan not only invaded Kashmir against the will of the people of Kashmir, it has so far violated every aspect of the UN Resolution, thus it cannot ask India now after 50 years to implement the resolution in only the 45 per cent of the original state of Jammu and Kashmir.

Pakistan so far has built airfields in the occupied territory, and imposed a full civilian and military control while claiming the territory as Azad Kashmir.

Pakistan, by a "Constitution Amendment", incorporated a part of Pakistan-held Kashmir that is, Northern Areas, in Pakistan thereby changing the territorial status of J&K and violating the UN Resolution.

Pakistan launched three large-scale operations on India in 1965, 1971 and the recent Kargil war in 1999 with [attacks

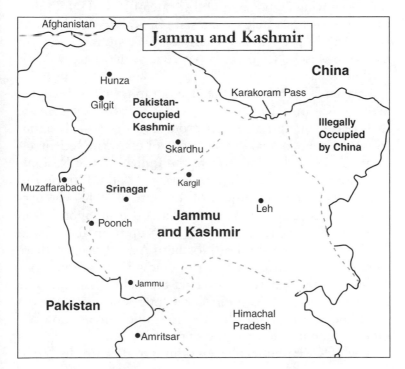

on] . . . J&K. Since 1988, Pakistan has sponsored cross-border terrorism in J&K aimed at changing the territorial status of J&K unilaterally, which is again [a] violation of the UN Resolution.

For these violations the UN could not impose sanctions on Pakistan, as the Resolution was not under Chapter VII of the UN Charter. . . .

The . . . type of resolution which does not fall in the purview of chapter seven needed cooperation of the concerned parties for their implementation. The UN resolutions on Kashmir do not fall in the category of chapter seven and hence required cooperation of the concerned parties for their implementation and in this case it is lacking.

China is illegally occupying [the] Aksai Chin area, which is 19 per cent of the territory. It will be next to impossible for the UN to make China vacate the area. To win Chinese support, Pakistan has gifted 4853 sq km of the Kashmiri territory in the Shakagam Valley to China in 1963, thus disrupting the territorial integrity of the state of J&K. China is now occupying 20 per cent of the state of J&K. UN Resolutions are for the whole of the state of J&K. With Pakistan occupying 35 per cent and China 20 per cent, it is absurd to call for plebiscite for only 45 per cent of the state, which is now in India. . . .

Pakistan has changed the demography of its occupied area in Kashmir by resettling large numbers of Punjabi ex-servicemen and Afghans from North-West Frontier Province, thereby making plebiscite of erstwhile J&K irrelevant. In 1992 all Hindus from the Indian part of Kashmir were forcibly expelled. There is large-scale infiltration of Pakistanis in the Indian part of the state of J&K. The percentage of Muslims in Ladakh went up from about 10 in 1947 to 46 in 2001; in Jammu it went up from about 20 in 1947 to 34 in 2001. In the "Northern Area Province" there were hardly any Muslims in 1947, now there are no non-Muslims either there or in Pakistan-held Kashmir. The original people of Kashmir have long since left, thus it would be next to impossible to determine who are now eligible to vote in the plebiscite as real Kashmiris.

The UN Resolutions have nothing to do with the "right

of self-determination" for the Kashmiris, because there are only two obvious options: join India or join Pakistan. There is no third option for "the independence", which most Muslim Kashmiris, according to the western media, want. If the Kashmiris wanted to join Pakistan, they could have done so in 1946 when Jinnah had invited Sheikh Abdullah to join Pakistan, which he had refused. Pakistan does not want to include the third option.

On 29 January 1994, the Jammu and Kashmir Liberation Front leader, Amanullah Khan, speaking in Muzaffarabad, reminded Pakistan Prime Minister Benazir Bhutto that Pakistan's persistent rejection of the third option of independence for Kashmir is "tantamount to denying the very right of self-determination" Pakistan has been harping on; a right, which, he asserted, cannot be limited, conditioned or circumscribed. But Pakistan's espousal of the right to self-determination has always been conditional and circumscribed.

The "right of self-determination" has many edges. Why should this right be only for the Muslim Kashmiris, when no other people in the British India of 1947 had that right? Ideally it should be applicable to all religions, tribes, sub-tribes, linguistic groups, etc. In that case, there will be hardly anything left in Pakistan (or in India or Bangladesh).

Also where should it start—is it for the whole country, every province of British India, every princely state, every district, every city, village? There is no clear limit. That is reason why most countries do not want to acknowledge the "right of self-determination" as a fundamental right because it will destroy the foundations of all nation states, including Pakistan.

Steps to Peace in Kashmir

Pakistan did not allow the "right of self-determination" for the people of the North-West Frontier Province, which was forced to join Pakistan, and all its leaders fled to Afghanistan in 1948. Neither Pakistan nor Bangladesh has allowed this right for the Chittagong Hill Area, where 97 per cent of the people were Buddhists in 1947. It was not applied either to the people of Chittral, Kafiristan, Hunza, Baltistan, Gilgit, Skardhu, where the majority of the people were not Muslims in 1947.

The fundamental question is, what do the vast majority of the Kashmiris want. Recently a very pro-Pakistani British politician Lord Eric Avebury asked an independent British market research company, Mori International, to conduct a survey in the Indian part of Kashmir. According to the result, the vast majority of Kashmiris oppose India and Pakistan going to war to find a permanent solution to the situation in Kashmir and believe the correct way to bring peace to the region is through democratic elections, ending violence, and economic development.

On the issue of citizenship, 61 per cent said they felt they would be better off politically and economically as Indian citizens and only six per cent as Pakistani citizens, but 33 per cent said they did not know. A very clear majority of the population—65 per cent—believes the presence of foreign militants in Jammu and Kashmir is damaging to the Kashmir cause, and most of the rest take the view that it is neither damaging nor helpful.

There is also widespread consensus on the types of proposals, which will help to bring about peace in Jammu and Kashmir. More than 85 per cent of the population, including at least 70 per cent in each region, think the following will help to bring about peace: (i) Economic development of the region to provide more job opportunities and reduction of poverty; (ii) The holding of free and fair elections to elect the people's representatives; (iii) Direct consultations between the Indian government and the people of Kashmir; (iv) An end to militant violence in the region; (v) Stopping the infiltration of militants across the Line of Control.

Western Bias Against India

The critical role people see for economic development in helping to solve the problems is further underlined by the 74 per cent who think that "people from outside of Kashmir being encouraged to invest in the area to help rebuild Kashmir's economy and tourist industry" will help to bring peace to the state. However, the western media has so far ignored the results of this survey. The western media and western academic circles have an implicit bias against India. . . . The problem, according to them, exists because India is not organising a plebiscite in Kashmir. A significant number of western (including Australian and Japanese) politicians have the same view. That is the exact reason why, except for the Soviet Union, no other country in the past has supported India's position.

The western media does not want to understand the logic of secularism; the reason why India cannot give Kashmir to Pakistan despite the fact it has a Muslim majority. The existence of Kashmir in India is the guarantee that Muslims in the rest of India can stay in India in a secular state.

| "*The militancy in Kashmir is part of a broad nationalist movement that wants a future free of both meddling powers.*"

Both India and Pakistan Have Mistreated the Kashmiri People

Mark Baker

Mark Baker is a reporter for *The Age*, a newspaper based in Melbourne, Australia. In the following viewpoint, he interviews several leading political figures in Kashmir and describes how the growing cycle of violence has devastated the region's economy and society. Baker argues that both Pakistan and India have victimized Kashmir and mistreated its people. Pakistan has used the region to fight a proxy war against India and has supported terrorists in the region. Indian forces, meanwhile, have behaved like an army of occupation in Kashmir and have subjected its people to numerous human rights abuses. The tragedy of Kashmir is that neither India nor Pakistan act in the best interests of Kashmir's people, Baker concludes.

As you read, consider the following questions:
1. How many lives have been lost from 1989 to 2002 due to armed forces fighting in Kashmir, according to Baker?
2. How is India to blame for the problems it faces in Kashmir, according to the author?
3. What disturbing implication does the author draw from the assassination of Abdul Ghani Lone, a Kashmiri separatist leader?

The boulevard beside the fabled Dal Lake is deserted, apart from some grazing cattle and a few forlorn souvenir stalls. Grand old houseboats are mostly empty and in disrepair. The lake itself is slowly dying, choked by an advancing tide of stinking weed and algae, the legacy of years of pollution and neglect.

This was once the peak tourist season in Srinagar, the time when thousands of travelers, from billionaires to budget trekkers, flocked to the Kashmir Valley to unwind amid the serenity of the lush green foothills of the Himalayas. Now the tourists have disappeared along with the jobs and prosperity they brought. Srinagar is now a city under siege in a brutal war zone. There are military checkpoints everywhere and fortified guard posts on most intersections. The streets are patrolled around the clock by trucks mounted with heavy machine guns and armored personnel carriers.

A Bitter Feud

For half a century Kashmir has been the center of a bitter territorial feud between India and Pakistan; for 13 years [since 1989] it has been gripped by a separatist uprising that has claimed more than 34,000 lives, and for the past two weeks [of May and June 2002], it has been the focus of global trepidation at the prospect of the world's first full-blown nuclear war. But as the military build-up continues on both sides of the Line of Control (LOC)—the U.N.-mandated boundary that separates the Indian and Pakistani halves of Kashmir—attention has scarcely focused on the history that has brought the two bitter rivals to the threshold of a fourth war since their partition at independence from Britain in 1947, this time under the menacing shadow of their newly acquired nuclear weapons.

India, which has threatened to attack Pakistan in response to a raid on a military base in Kashmir two weeks ago [in May 2002] in which 34 were killed, and the assault on the Indian Parliament last December [2001] that left 14 dead, has won widespread international sympathy as a victim of terrorism. There has also been almost universal acceptance of New Delhi's assertion that the root cause of the problem is Pakistan's active support for militants infiltrating across the LOC.

This simplistic line—readily digested in the black-and-white world of post-Sept. 11 [terrorist attacks on America] politics—largely ignores the extent to which India has been architect of its own predicament. Equally, it ignores the fact that, while Pakistan has for years used Kashmir to fight a proxy war against India, at its heart the militancy in Kashmir is part of a broad nationalist movement that wants a future free of both meddling powers.

While acknowledging the provocation of Pakistan's long-standing support for terrorist groups and their tactics, George Perkovich, a senior associate at the Carnegie Endowment for International Peace, says: "India's failure to offer decent governance and constructive engagement with Kashmiri dissidents created the current mess. . . ."

A Long Struggle

The present crisis can be traced back to independence in 1947 when India seized the Kashmir Valley and its hinterland, promising the Muslim-majority population a plebiscite on their future, a promise that was never honored. The conflict turned violent in 1989 after years of corrupt and patronizing misrule from New Delhi, the rigging of elections to exclude nationalist candidates from power, and growing repression and human-rights abuses.

"For 40 years our people waged a peaceful and democratic struggle," says professor Abdul Ghani Bhat, chairman of the All Parties Hurriyat Conference, an alliance of more than 20 separatist parties and groups. "It only turned violent after the Indians chose not to hear the heartbeat of the people and came down heavily on people waging a just . . . struggle."

The cycle of violence has grown steadily worse over the past decade, with the Indian government responding to attacks on its forces by sending in more troops—estimated to total more than 500,000 before the latest border buildup—and cracking down harder on real and imagined threats.

In a report released in May 2002, Amnesty International said an average of 100 people a month were killed by security forces and in indiscriminate attacks on civilian and military targets. "Hundreds of cases of torture, deaths in custody, extrajudicial executions, and 'disappearances' are reported every year," the report said. "In most cases, no one is held to account for such human-rights violations."

While its forces behave like an army of occupation, the government in New Delhi and its notoriously corrupt surrogate state administration treats the local population with contempt. Kashmir remains one of the most under-resourced states in India. There are no mobile telephone facilities in the state, and after the attack on Parliament last December 2001 . . . telephone and Internet links were cut.

"Everything is now gone: security, order, honor," says Bhat. "All structure of civilized life has come tumbling down amid the roar of guns. . . . It is only the law of the jungle that prevails." He argues that the separatist alliance does not condone terrorism but understands the motivation of "freedom fighters" opposing Indian rule.

Two Kashmir Problems

There are actually two Kashmir problems, deeply linked but distinctive. Both are real and long-lasting problems. Both are insoluble if tackled alone, but risk causing more damage if intertwined too closely together. First, what happens to the state of Jammu and Kashmir? Should it be given to India or to Pakistan, become independent, or be repartitioned? This Kashmir problem has kept lawyers, diplomats, and writers busy since 1947. . . . This problem has become rather abstract, debated by one country—Pakistan—that has usually spoken about the past without reference to the present, and by another—India—that talks about Kashmir only in the present (post-1971) without reference to the past. To outsiders, the issue is reduced simply to geography and geopolitics.

The second Kashmiri problem is far more complicated, interesting, and pressing—the problem of Kashmiris themselves. How do Kashmiris get the government they want? The origins of the militancy that has since 1988 claimed more than 35,000 lives lie here. Yet this can be the only source of an enduring solution.

Alexander Evans, *Washington Quarterly*, Spring 2001.

Moderate Kashmiri politician Mehbooba Mufti, whose father was the Congress Party national home affairs minister in the early 1990s, says India is largely responsible for the present crisis: "They treat us like a colony. . . . Everything is derided by Delhi. People cannot elect their own representatives. Every election has been rigged from the first one in 1951." She says the international community is putting too much emphasis on calls for Pakistan to halt cross-border infiltration. "The question is not how sincere President [Pervez] Musharraf is, but how much power he has to control the situation. Pakistan must seek to stop the infiltration to ease tensions, but the Indian government must also take concrete steps to bring about a dialogue."

Spread of Terrorism

The assassination of Abdul Ghani Lone—a separatist leader prepared to negotiate a compromise settlement with India—is seen as evidence that the terrorism in Kashmir has moved beyond the capacity of either India or Pakistan to quickly bring it under control. "The pan-Islamic jihadis (holy warriors) are pushing India and Pakistan toward conflict as part of their plan to polarize the region between Muslim and non-Muslim," says political commentator Husain Haqqani, a former adviser to the Bhutto and Sharif governments in Pakistan. The killing is also seen as evidence that the militants, estimated to number as many as 3,000, and some of whom are Arabs and Chechens linked to [terrorist] Osama bin Laden's Al-Qaeda network, will not only ignore directions from Pakistan but will also fight any attempts by moderate Kashmiris to reach a peace deal.

Bhat says the Hurriyat parties are willing to be flexible and consider a wide range of possible outcomes if India is prepared to sit down and negotiate a solution to the crisis. One possibility, he says, is that both Indian and Pakistani troops withdraw from their parts of Kashmir under U.N. supervision and allow the establishment of an interim administration pending a referendum on the future of the territory after five years.

The problem is that India has shown no willingness to compromise over Kashmir in the past 50 years, and so far, there is little evidence that the United States and its allies are ready to acknowledge that New Delhi's conduct in Kashmir is fundamental to the present crisis, let alone pressure India to honor the right to self-determination. And there is equal skepticism that Pakistan is about to surrender its political leverage in Kashmir.

Kashmir Held Hostage

"We are being held hostage by these two nations," says Sajad Ghani Lone, the son of the assassinated politician. "Kashmir's interests do not converge with the interests of India and Pakistan. They only look at us in terms of miles of territory. . . ." The pessimists' view is that peace is as distant as ever for Kashmir because both Pakistan and India have powerful reasons for maintaining the conflict—provided it can be kept at a level short of outright war. Some analysts in Pakistan believe the uprising in Kashmir during the past decade has given Islamabad defense on the cheap with a relative handful of militants tying up more than half a million Indian troops. For India, others argue, Kashmir is justification for maintaining the power elite that has grown up around one of the world's biggest armies.

"A lot of people have a vested interest in ensuring the problem of Kashmir is never solved," says Sajad Ghani Lone. "It is a huge moneymaking machine. It's big business with guaranteed profits: The more killing there is, the more money you make. Kashmir is about power and money. That is Kashmir's sorrow."

Periodical Bibliography

The following articles have been selected to supplement the diverse views presented in this chapter.

Aasim Sajjad Akhtar
"The Democracy Killers," *New Internationalist*, September 2002.

Anto Akkara
"India's Christians Face Continued Threats," *Christianity Today*, February 12, 2001.

Richard Behar
"Kidnapped Nation: Welcome to Pakistan, America's Frontline Ally in the War on Terror, Where Culture and Economy Conspire Against Even the Best Intentions," *Fortune*, April 29, 2002.

Hannah Bloch
"Blaming the Victim: Can a Raped Woman Be Stoned for Adultery? In Pakistan, It's Possible," *Time*, May 27, 2002.

BusinessWeek
"Pakistan's Referendum," May 6, 2002.

Neera Chowdhury
"In J&K, a Chance for Everybody," *Indian Express*, October 14, 2002. http://iecolumnists.expressindia.com.

Economist
"One Election That Wasn't Rigged: Kashmir and Pakistan," October 12, 2002.

Alexander Evans
"Reducing Tension Is Not Enough," *Washington Quarterly*, Spring 2001.

Ghulam Nabi Fai
"Are Kashmiris Fundamentalist, Secessionist Terrorists?" *Washington Report on Middle East Affairs*, March 2002.

Laura D. Jenkins
"Becoming Backward: Preferential Policies and Religious Minorities in India," *Journal of Commonwealth & Comparative Politics*, July 2001.

Rod Nordland
"Pakistan: Of Tribes, Trials, and Tribulations," *Newsweek*, August 5, 2002.

Martha Nussbaum
"Sex, Laws, and Inequality: What India Can Teach the United States," *Daedalus*, Winter 2002.

Surinder Oberot
"Kashmir: Caught in the Crossfire," *Bulletin of the Atomic Scientists*, September/October 1998.

Jeff Sellers
"High Court Injustice," *Christianity Today*, November 12, 2001.

Vijayashri Sripati	"Human Rights in India—Fifty Years After Independence," *Denver Journal of International Law and Policy*, Fall 1997.
Nagarajan Vittal	"Corruption and the State," *Harvard International Review*, Fall 2001.
Neena Vyas	"It's Time to Draw the Line," *Hindu*, January 20, 2002. www.hinduonnet.com/thehindu.

CHAPTER 3

How Should the World Community Treat India and Pakistan?

Chapter Preface

As the world's second-most populous nation, its largest democracy, and a possessor of nuclear arms, India is becoming one of the world's most powerful countries. Despite India's rising influence, however, the nation has been denied a permanent seat on the United Nations (UN) Security Council, arguably the most important organ of the UN. The council's refusal to grant India a permanent seat has generated much controversy, both within India and around the world.

The UN is the world's most powerful peacekeeping organization. Composed of more than thirty organizations from around the world, the UN works to solve problems that challenge humanity, such as war, poverty, and human rights abuses. The UN Security Council has the primary responsibility for the maintenance of international peace and security. To fulfill its mission, the council has the power to investigate disputes between nations, formulate plans for resolving such disputes, or take military action against aggressors. Such wide-ranging powers make the Security Council a feared and respected presence internationally.

Presently, the five permanent council seats belong to the United States, Russia, China, the United Kingdom, and France. As permanent members, each of these nations wields the power to veto any council action. India has questioned why the United Kingdom and France—who have 5 percent of India's population—are allowed permanent seats while India is not. In March 2002, A. Gopinathan, India's deputy representative to the UN, demanded that the Security Council allow India to have a permanent seat. He complained that although council peacekeeping efforts were increasingly made on behalf of and between developing nations, those nations—such as India—had not been given a proportionate voice on the council. He cautioned that the "unrepresentative and anachronistic" character of the council might hamper its ability to negotiate international peace.

Philip Oldenburg, associate director of the Southern Asia Institute at Columbia University, sympathizes with India's position: "Today, [India is] every bit the equal, and then some, of Britain or France, be it militarily, economically or politically." He notes that India has tremendous influence in South Asia, claiming that Indians "basically govern or have great influence over a billion and a half people." Other commentators point out that India's economy has grown significantly—its gross domestic product has grown eightfold over the past three decades—and will continue to expand.

However, many nations around the world agree with the council that India should be denied a permanent seat. These countries contend that India experiences too much inner strife resulting from human rights violations to be considered a permanent member of the world's most powerful peacekeeping organization. They cite India's caste system, recurring Muslim-Hindu riots, and India's oppression of the Kashmiri people—who want independence from India—as evidence of India's growing unconcern for human rights. Other council supporters claim that India's decision to expand its nuclear arms program illustrates why it would make an unsuitable permanent member of the council, whose responsibilities include reducing nuclear proliferation. Pakistan's ambassador to the UN, Shamshad Ahmad, argues, "The Security Council is under obligation of recent resolutions following India's nuclear tests [in 1998] not to reward India for having nuclearized the South Asian region." Pakistan's stance is understandable—as India's long-standing enemy, the less powerful nation would naturally oppose any resolution giving India more international prestige and enhancing its influence in South Asia.

It remains to be seen whether the UN Security Council will enact reforms that will enable India to see its ambitions for a permanent seat fulfilled. As India grows more powerful, it quite naturally wants a larger say in world affairs and increased recognition of its strength. The authors in the following chapter debate how the international community should treat India and Pakistan. To be sure, both countries promise to figure prominently on the world stage in the years to come.

> "The current [terrorist] situation requires
> Western nations to reach out to Muslim
> states like Pakistan who have not
> historically been strong allies."

The United States Should Treat Pakistan as an Ally Against Terrorism

Melissa Dell

Melissa Dell contends in the following viewpoint that the United States should seek an alliance with Pakistan to fight the war against terrorism despite Pakistan's reputation for harboring terrorists. She points out that many of the world's terrorist acts are being committed by extremists in Muslim countries and that an ally in Central Asia would help stabilize the region. Dell warns that rather than the short-term commitments made by the United States in the past—which often left Muslim nations at the mercy of ruthless dictators—an American alliance with Pakistan should be long-term. Melissa Dell is a staff writer for the *Harvard International Review*.

As you read, consider the following questions:
1. According to Dell, where do the roots of Pakistani extremism lie?
2. What are some of the similarities between Afghanistan and the Weimar Republic of Germany, in the author's opinion?
3. As stated by the author, how much money has the United States, Japan, and Europe pledged to combat the Afghan refugee crisis?

Melissa Dell, "Learning Curve: The United States and the Future of Pakistan," *Harvard International Review*, Spring 2002, pp. 34–37. Copyright © 2002 by *Harvard International Review*. Reproduced by permission.

Since the terrorist attacks in New York and Washington on September 11, 2001, coalition building has become the new catchphrase in foreign policy. Forming close relationships with Muslim countries is essential for success in the war on terrorism, and thus the West has looked to President Pervez Musharraf of Pakistan as a key ally. However, many find it ironic and even appalling that one of the West's primary allies in the war on terrorism is a country that has had a reputation for harboring terrorists, given that the Taliban has been instrumental in providing support for Pakistani militants in their quasi-war in Kashmir. The West needs Pakistan as an ally, but in order to avoid unpleasant future consequences, it is necessary that this alliance develop into a long-term relationship and not remain merely a solution to present problems. . . .

Coalition Building

There is no doubt that the West needs the support of Muslim states in the war on terrorism, but policy-makers must carefully consider the foreign-policy blunders made in Afghanistan. The West, and the United States in particular, has a long history of willfully ignoring the authoritarian tendencies of potential allies. Western donors certainly had no scruples in supporting the *mujahideen* movement, despite its radical tendencies.[1] Neither did most feel any compunction against withdrawing all support once the direct Soviet threat diminished.

Some fear that the West is once again sacrificing the spirit of democracy in order to entice Muslim nations to join the anti-terrorism coalition. In exchange for President Musharraf's cooperation, the United States has agreed to forgive the Pakistani debt and lift sanctions imposed after Pakistan's nuclear tests. As London's *Guardian* newspaper editorialized, "The assumption of wrath over nuclear proliferation vanished with the economic sanctions imposed on Islamabad [Pakistan]. The West's supposed love for democracy, manifest when more sanctions greeted General Pervez Mushar-

---

1. The Mujahideen were fighters in Afghanistan whom the United States aided in the 1980s in order to contest Soviet occupation in that country.

raf's military coup, is also declared null and void. When and if the Afghan crisis subsides, he will be back to crisis as usual—but this time with some sparkling new weaponry, courtesy of the Yanks, and his bomb internationally sanctified. The 'war' against terrorism will cement army rule for as long as it lasts." Many Pakistanis view their country as a failed state, fearing that, if left to itself, the collusion between armed extremists and elements of the government would further Pakistan's reputation as a safe haven for terrorists.

It is certainly not ideal for US military and government officials to receive much of their intelligence in the war on terrorism from a government that is itself notorious for harboring terrorists. When viewed from this angle, it would seem as if an alliance with Pakistan could be counterproductive in the attempt to eradicate terrorism. Yet it is imperative to consider whether the need for Pakistani intelligence and support in the continued struggle against terrorism outweighs the oppressive and radical tendencies of the Pakistani government. If so, what should be the policy toward Pakistan now that the war on terrorism in Afghanistan is winding down?

Many of the problems that led to the current situation in Afghanistan are also present in Pakistan. The roots of extremism and terrorism in Pakistan lie in its precipitous economic decline, lack of representative institutions, and meager civil liberties and human rights. The September 2001 crisis placed President Musharraf in a delicate position between US demands to support military action against Afghanistan and the threat of civil conflict from important sectors of Pakistani society sympathetic to the Taliban. There certainly is a faction within Pakistani society that feels betrayed by the United States.

Although there is doubt about the legitimacy of these claims, they are potentially explosive extremist sentiments. As oppressive as Musharraf's regime may be, many policymakers have an even greater fear of the regime that would come to power if he were defeated. An extremist regime with nuclear weapons certainly does not bode well for the region's future. This places global policy-makers in an extremely precarious situation, and the elections that Musharraf has promised to hold in 2003 further raise the stakes. On the one hand, the elections provide an unprecedented opportunity for greater openness within the Pakistani government and would allow the country to take the first steps toward democracy. On the other hand, if sentiments become too polarized, an extremist regime could ascend to power, worsening the plight of the Pakistani people.

Safe for Democracy?

Certainly the failed practice of appeasement in the years prior to World War II is at the back of many minds. At the same time, most everyone is in support of coalition building, and nobody argues that the eradication of terrorism is not a noble goal. It is interesting to note the similarities between Afghanistan and the Weimar Republic of Germany. Both were ravaged by economic upheaval, both experienced a profound feeling of betrayal, and both fell victim to extremist authoritarian regimes that provided stability in times of adversity. The United States, Britain, and France put aside their differences with the Soviet Union to protect Western Europe, Asia, and the rest of the world from the forces of oppression. The United States and its Western allies are still trying—as they were during the Cold War and World War II—to pursue these same goals.

Pakistan Is Vital to the United States

The survival of Pakistan in its existing form is a vital U.S. security interest, one that trumps all other American interests in the country. A collapse of Pakistan—into internal anarchy or an Islamist revolution—would cripple the global campaign against Islamist terrorism. Strengthening the Pakistani state and cementing its cooperation with the West have thus become immensely important to Washington.

Anatol Lieven, *Foreign Affairs*, January/February 2002.

This leaves foreign policy-makers to ponder the proper role of Western nations. The answer to the foreign-policy predicament in Pakistan is dependent on whether the war on terrorism is a war on the state level and revolving primarily around military action, an ideological war, or a combination of both. If it is to be a purely ideological war, it would be extremely dubious to have allies who harbor terrorists themselves. Yet conducting an entirely ideological war is not practical. The current situation requires Western nations to reach out to Muslim states like Pakistan who have not historically been strong allies. Neither can the fight be purely on the state level, since terrorism transcends national boundaries. Rather, it should be a combination of both, combating terrorism on a concrete, national level while encouraging democracy and civil rights on a more ideological level.

Although Pakistan does have a history of harboring terrorists, its recent alliance with the West is a huge step toward recognizing the ills of terrorism abroad. Since September 2001, Musharraf's government has condemned terrorist attacks and arrested leaders of the Jaish-e-Mohammed and Lashkar-e-Taiba terrorist networks. While US President George W. Bush acknowledges that there is still additional work to be done, especially with regard to state-sanctioned terrorism in the Kashmir region, he argues that Musharraf is indeed moving forward. In fact, this alliance could be the first step in correcting Pakistan's political instability, nuclear proliferation, and human-rights abuses. At the same time, it provides an excellent opportunity to hold Musharraf's regime to its promise to have elections in 2003.

Long-Term Commitments

Not only humanitarian aid but also opportunities for education in such fields as business development, teaching, technology, and health care will help foster long-standing coalitions and make democracy a much more plausible alternative. It is true that military action is sometimes necessary, but as conflicts from World War I through the Soviet invasion of Afghanistan demonstrate, military force by itself is not a long-term solution. Rather, the problems that plague Central Asia and the Middle East are long-term and will require equally long-term alliances and commitments. Although it might be easier to simply move on once short-term goals are accomplished, ongoing aid along the lines of programs mentioned above is essential.

Western policy-makers are on the right track in developing such alliances. US Secretary of State Colin Powell, in a recent visit to both Afghanistan and Pakistan, pledged that victory in the war will be followed by an equally determined campaign to rebuild Afghanistan: "We will be there. We will not abandon them." The new interim leader of Afghanistan, Hamid Karzai, believes the United States is committed: "Now I can tell [the Afghan people], 'yes, the US will stay with us.'"

The United Nations and Western governments have pledged to work closely with the Pakistani government on the Afghan refugee situation. Hundreds of thousands of refugees are in desperate need of supplies, and the UN High Commission for Refugees, led by Ruud Lubbers, hopes that this time it will receive the support it needs from the Western nations in order to be successful in combating the refugee crisis. Western donors have stated their long-term commitment; at the recent Tokyo conference, the United States, Japan, and Europe pledged US$1.3 billion of the total US$3.9 billion raised by the conference.

Although terrorism will never be entirely eradicated, establishing lasting, mutual, and collaborative alliances with the Muslim nations, including Musharraf's regime, is one step in the right direction. It is imperative not to lose sight of the fact that this partnership has real unprecedented potential to bring stability to Central Asia.

"*[Pakistani leaders] are committed to the
notion of an 'Islamic Bomb,' and . . . have
maintained ties to the international
network of radical Islamic groups.*"

The United States Should Not Treat Pakistan as an Ally Against Terrorism

Leon Hadar

In the following viewpoint, Leon Hadar argues that Pakistan
has a history of aiding terrorist groups and should not be
viewed as an ally in America's war against terrorism. According to Hadar, Pakistan helped leaders of the Taliban regime—
which the United States has accused of supporting the terrorist organization al-Qaeda—during America's war against
terrorism in Afghanistan in 2001. Hadar asserts that Pakistan is a nuclear dictatorship committed to supporting Islamic radicals and should not be trusted. Leon Hadar is a research fellow in foreign policy studies at the Cato Institute,
a libertarian public policy research foundation.

As you read, consider the following questions:
1. What nations has President George W. Bush called the
   "Axis of Evil," according to Hadar?
2. In the author's opinion, how did Iran help the United
   States fight the war against terrorism?
3. How have nations belonging to the "Axis of Evil"
   cooperated with the United States in regards to nuclear
   weapons, as reported by the author?

P resident George W. Bush has declared that the next phase of the anti-terrorism campaign would be aimed at pressing Iraq, Iran, and North Korea—the so-called Axis of Evil—not to develop chemical, biological and nuclear weapons. He also stressed in his State of the Union Address that the war against terrorism would be grounded in a set of universal values, including the rule of law, religious freedom and respect for women.

The "Axis" of Evil

Much of the commentary that followed Bush's speech raised questions about why he lumped together Baghdad, Teheran and Pyongyang, which, after all, have different political systems and divergent foreign policy goals. A more intriguing mystery, though, concerns a country that was missing from the list: Pakistan. Islamabad, Pakistan, should have been placed at the center of the "axis," not only because of its close ties to radical Muslim terrorist groups and its efforts to acquire weapons of mass destruction, but because its anti-Western and militant Islamic orientation is the antithesis to the universal values that the Bush administration is supposedly promoting as part of its foreign policy.

But instead of being placed on President Bush's list of evil states, Pakistan is now topping America's "A List" of the antiterrorism coalition. The garden-variety dictatorship in Baghdad, Iraq, the reformist government in Teheran, Iran, and the detente-oriented North Korea are being marginalized and punished by Washington and compared to Nazi Germany and the Soviet Union. But Pakistan's military dictator, General Pervez Musharraf, who brought an end to his nation's short democratic experience and has advanced Pakistan's nuclearization program, while promoting ties to radical Islamic groups at home and abroad, is being praised by U.S. officials for his "courage" and "vision." And he was a guest of honor at the White House.

Pakistan's government, led by an unreliable military clique that is assisting radical Islamic terrorist groups in Kashmir, pressing for a war with India, and presiding over a corrupt and mismanaged economy, has been a recipient of vast sums of U.S. military and financial aid.

Pakistan's Support of the Taliban

One should recall that it was America's "friend" Pakistan that, through its military-religious nexus, led by its infamous intelligence services, provided the Taliban fighters with the military aid that helped bring them to power in Kabul in 1994 and create the anti-American terrorist state of Afghanistan.

Ganguli. © by *Business India*. Reprinted with permission.

At the same time, the "evil" Iran was a regional adversary of the Taliban regime and one of the leading backers of the Northern Alliance opposition forces [who fought against the Taliban]. Moreover, despite Washington's hostile attitude and its efforts to isolate Iran diplomatically and economically, Tehran agreed to give indirect logistical support to the American military campaign in Afghanistan and cooperated with effort to oust the Taliban. Pakistan, on the other hand, joined the American-led coalition only after enormous U.S. diplomatic and military pressure and in exchange for increasing American aid. In fact, while the Iranians were helping their Northern Alliance allies in their war against the Taliban after [the September 11, 2001, terrorist attacks on America], Pakistani military and intelligence services were assisting the losing Taliban fighters and evacuating thousands of them into Pakistan.

Although the Bush Administration should certainly continue monitoring the efforts of Iraq, Iran and North Korea to acquire or develop weapons of mass destruction and should take every measure to prevent the transfer of such military technology to terrorists, it's important to remember that these three nations have agreed to open some of their weapons-production sites to international inspection. Most experts agree that it will take several years for Iraq and Iran to develop nuclear military capability and that neither those two countries nor North Korea have provided weapons of mass destruction (WMD) technology to Al-Qaeda [believed to be responsible for the September 11 attacks] or other terrorist networks. If anything, the Bush administration's concern with nuclear proliferation and with the possible transfer of WMD to terrorist groups should make Pakistan—a nuclear military power, whose military leaders and scientists are committed to the notion of an "Islamic Bomb," and who have maintained ties to the international network of radical Islamic groups, including Al-Qaeda—a focus of U.S. antiproliferation and antiterrorism policies.

Pakistan Is Not an Ally

No, Pakistan shouldn't be branded as "evil" and subject to a campaign of diplomatic isolation and military confrontation that the Bush administration seems to be directing against Iraq, Iran and North Korea. But neither should Pakistan be lauded as America's strategic ally in the war against terrorism and be the recipient of U.S. military and economic aid.

> "Benefits to U.S. national security interests would occur on a global scale if the United States and India became strategic partners."

The United States Should Treat India as an Ally

Victor M. Gobarev

Victor M. Gobarev is an independent security policy analyst based in Washington, D.C. Gobarev argues in the following viewpoint that the United States should view India as a potential friend rather than a potential enemy. He urges the United States to accept India's nuclear power status, contending that India will use its missiles strictly for defensive purposes. In addition, Gobarev maintains that America should officially recognize India's world power status by voting to give it a seat on the United Nations Security Council. Developing stronger ties with India would help protect U.S. security interests and improve the American economy, he argues.

As you read, consider the following questions:

1. According to the author, what nation does India consider the greatest threat to its national security?
2. How should the United States justify its acceptance of India's nuclear power status, as stated by Gobarev?
3. In the author's opinion, what would be the most notable benefit to U.S. national security interests of developing better relations with India?

Victor M. Gobarev, "India as a World Power: Changing Washington's Myopic Policy," *Policy Analysis*, September 11, 2000, pp. 1, 12–13, 20–22. Copyright © 2000 by The Cato Institute. Reproduced by permission.

A merican interest in and concerns about India rose sharply after that country carried out underground nuclear tests in May 1998. Clinton administration officials belatedly acknowledged that developing a good working relationship with India should be one of America's top foreign policy priorities. President Bill Clinton's visit to South Asia in March 2000 was an important symbolic step.

Mistakes in U.S. Policy

That initiative, however, does not constitute a major breakthrough in relations between India and the United States. Paying greater attention to India, although long overdue, cannot by itself dramatically improve uneasy U.S.-Indian relations and turn India into a de facto strategic partner. The fundamental mistake made by U.S. leaders has been to underestimate India and its economic and military potential. How India uses its growing power can either enhance or seriously undermine U.S. interests. Continued insistence by the United States that India liquidate its nuclear arsenal will only cause major problems in relations between Washington and New Delhi.

Washington's overemphasis on the proliferation issue illustrates the tendency of U.S. policymakers to treat India as a potential adversary rather than a potential friend. U.S. leaders should not insist on improvement in New Delhi's human rights record in Kashmir, or set other preconditions, for the U.S.-Indian relationship. Pursuing the current course may well extend the impasse in relations to the point of irrevocably "losing" India.

Mistakes in U.S. policy have contributed to India's drifting toward a Russia-India-China nexus aimed at preventing U.S. global domination. The likelihood of India's participation in an anti-U.S. alliance will depend on what New Delhi thinks about American geopolitical designs toward India and its national security interests.

A long-range strategy needs to be based on Washington's willingness to accept India's world power status. That means accepting India into the club of nuclear weapons states and enthusiastically endorsing New Delhi's bid for permanent membership in the UN Security Council. The main benefit to the United States of such a breakthrough in U.S.-Indian relations would be to prevent a dramatic adverse change in the current global geopolitical situation, which currently favors the United States. An assertive India could help stabilize the Persian Gulf and Central Asian regions. Even more important, India could become a strategic counterweight to China and a crucial part of a stable balance of power in both East Asia and South Asia. . . .

India's Nuclear Arsenal

For India, the nuclear arsenal is an integral part of world power status. Fortunately for the rest of the world, India's nuclear weapons program seems defensive. . . . Prime Minister Atal Behari Vajpayee confirmed that he had repeated in his private meeting with President Clinton India's commitment not to conduct further nuclear explosive tests and not to be the first to use nuclear weapons. He also added that India's nuclear program "has always been defensive in nature" and would remain so, but that the program is necessary.

American experts assume that India is developing its nuclear program to check hostile Pakistani (and possibly Chinese) ambitions. But there is much more to it than that. India is developing its "minimal" nuclear deterrence for purposes that for the most part have little to do with Pakistan. India can successfully deter Pakistan, which is no match for India's military, by using its superiority in conventional forces.

New Delhi's real goal is to have a sufficient arsenal to deter *any* aggressor, even the most powerful country in the world. The Indians do worry about a nuclear-armed China. During President Clinton's visit, Prime Minster Vajpayee said it was not "realistic" for India to give up its nuclear weapons in the face of Pakistan's nuclear proliferation and China's nuclear might. But it is the United States, with its global reach and superior power, that India wants to deter. New Delhi is apprehensive about possible U.S. plans to attack India. Primarily because of that uneasiness India will not give up its nuclear weapons program. That decision is an unspoken truth that Indian officials never publicly acknowledge in their talks with American officials for two reasons:

first, because of cultural habits Indians are not accustomed to telling a foreigner something that might be seen as an offense; and second, Indians do not want a public statement about a U.S. "threat" to ruin chances of improving U.S.-Indian relations.

Fear of U.S. Power and Intentions

If one reads between the lines of Indian public statements, apprehension about possible hostile moves by the United States toward India can be clearly discerned. To give a recent example, President Kocheril Raman Narayanan visited France in late April 2000. He and French prime minister Lionel Jospin agreed (in a none-too-subtle reference to the United States) that a single superpower should not dominate the world.

The NATO bombing of Yugoslavia, continuing U.S. missile attacks on Iraq, and missile strikes on targets in Sudan and Afghanistan have all served to reinforce India's fears. It should be noticed that India considers not one but three foreign countries (Pakistan, China, and the United States) as potential adversaries. The United States, the most powerful and dangerous from India's perspective, has moved to the head of the list of "priority" threats because of the U.S.-led military coercion of Serbia over Kosovo.

Thus, at its core, India's determination to keep its nuclear weapons until universal nuclear disarmament has little to do with Pakistan, much to do with China, and everything to do with America. This Indian view may seem entirely unreasonable to most Americans. But if the United States wants to dramatically improve relations with India, it cannot build them on false assumptions. The United States must recognize that Indian leaders (and much of the population) consider America the most serious potential foreign threat and that Washington cannot dismiss such Indian security concerns and conduct a successful policy in South Asia. Many discussions held by the author throughout India with various representatives of India's political and military elites during the 1990s have one thing in common: Indians still distrust the United States and fear that one day they may be subject to an American attack. . . .

A reactive policy toward India (e.g., New Delhi tests a nuclear bomb, Washington imposes sanctions) is easy to conduct but regrettably shortsighted. A proactive policy—building a long-term strategic relationship with India—is hard to pursue but the only approach likely to succeed. There is no quick solution for improving U.S.-Indian relations. The only feasible way for improvement is for America to accept India's world power status. That, in turn, will require daring foreign policy moves designed to bring India closer to the United States and its national interests.

Rogue Countries, India, and Nuclear Weapons

The most radical move the United States could make for dramatic improvement in its relations with India would be to unconditionally accept India's nuclear status. The United States should formally recognize India's joining the nuclear club and ask all other members of the club to do the same.

The U.S. official statement on the matter should be explicit. The statement should emphasize the defensive nature of India's nuclear weapons program and the lack of any Indian offensive threat to other countries. An explicit dividing line should be drawn between democratic India and rogue countries whose weapons of mass destruction (WMD) threaten the world. Moreover, it should be specified that America's formal recognition of India's nuclear status is an exception to Washington's general opposition to proliferation.

The justification for making an exception in India's case should not be based on the fact that India already has nuclear weapons, since that justification could be used as an excuse by some so-called nuclear threshold rogue countries to justify their nuclear weapons programs. Instead, the reasoning should be based on the undeniable fact that India is a stable democracy with a solid record of aversion to the use of military power for aggression. The statement should also emphasize that this well-deserved international reputation, and the moral authority it garners, puts India beyond any reasonable suspicion that it would use nuclear weapons for purposes other than retaliation against a nuclear attack.

The concerns that such a move would invite increased nuclear proliferation do not seem justified. Rogue countries currently working on acquiring nuclear weapons will continue to do so independently of U.S. recognition of India's nuclear status. Moreover, many states, especially in the Third World, would welcome a conciliatory move as evidence that the United States wishes to pursue an equitable foreign and international security policy for all nations, not merely for developed countries. Britain, France, Russia, and China, the members of the nuclear club, are likely to follow the U.S. move. Russia and China would be outmaneuvered, since a crucial foreign policy and international security initiative dealing with India would have passed from them to America. That move would also deal a heavy blow to those in China, Russia, and India itself who dream of building the tripartite strategic alliance to oppose the United States.

An Ally Against Terrorism

Far from being a reluctant partner, India is a committed U.S. ally. Within a week of the September 11 [terrorist] attacks, India provided the U.S. with intelligence on the locations of more than 120 terrorist training camps in Afghanistan. And in a nationwide address to India's one billion citizens, Indian Prime Minister Atal Behari Vajpayee proclaimed that America's war was India's as well, and offered the U.S. military immediate, unconditional use of several Indian air bases and port facilities.

H. Sterling Burnett and Wess Mitchell, nationalreview.com, December 12, 2001.

U.S. recognition of India as a nuclear power would remove the main obstacle to making America and India friends and de facto strategic partners. Such an initiative by Washington would likely mean India's acceptance of U.S. proposals on nonproliferation of WMD technology and fissile materials. India would join international talks on ending the production of fissile materials for nuclear weapons and would install effective controls for nuclear-related materials. Those measures would reduce the threat of proliferation from India and begin U.S.-Indian cooperation on counterproliferation.

At the same time that America admits India to the nuclear club, Washington should formally recognize India's world power status. In a major foreign policy statement Washington should formally recognize India's world status and global interests. Further, the United States should propose, and wholeheartedly support, India's candidacy for a permanent seat in the UN Security Council. Such actions would cause positive reactions around the world, since India is regarded as a leader of developing nations. Not only would U.S. international prestige increase, but countries such as Russia, China, and France would lose the initiative in the diplomatic struggle for India's favor. . . .

The Winning U.S. Policy on India

What would a [more effective] policy win for the United States? America would get a strategic partner of the highest caliber. Most important, such a policy would dramatically shift the global, geopolitical, and geostrategic balance in favor of the United States.

The geopolitical balance in Asia would be especially tilted in America's favor. India could help the United States contain expansionist threats from China to maintain order and stability in East and Southeast Asia. In addition, America would move further from the brink of nuclear confrontation with China over the Taiwan issue and other potential sources of friction. China would be less able to contemplate a confrontation with either its neighbors in East Asia or with the United States if Beijing had to worry about India's response.

Benefits to U.S. national security interests would occur on a global scale if the United States and India became strategic partners. Most notably, there would be no chance for an anti-U.S. Russia-India-China alliance. Preventing that outcome alone would be a huge geopolitical success for the United States. Further, effectiveness of U.S. intelligence and special operations against major international terrorist groups located in Afghanistan and Pakistan would significantly increase thanks to direct U.S.-Indian cooperation.

In response to eliminating sanctions and further opening our market to Indian goods, India would likely decrease import tariffs, securing easier access for American goods there. The American economy would benefit from enhanced trade and investment with India.

A foreign policy and national security strategy based on Washington's willingness to accept India's world power status, including accepting New Delhi in the nuclear club, is the only realistic way for a breakthrough in U.S.-Indian ties. The current bankrupt U.S. policy will merely extend stagnation in relations to the point of irrevocably losing India.

*"Washington should not be swayed . . .
into placing India's interests before
U.S. national security concerns."*

The United States Should Treat India as a Potential Security Threat

Larry M. Wortzel and Dana R. Dillon

Larry M. Wortzel is director and Dana R. Dillon is a policy analyst on Southeast Asia in the Asian Studies Center at the Heritage Foundation, a conservative think tank. In the following viewpoint, Wortzel and Dillon contend that the United States should not make agreements with India that would jeopardize U.S. national security. The authors maintain that India should be viewed as a grave security threat because of its ongoing efforts to develop more sophisticated nuclear weapons. Wortzel and Dillon believe that India is using its nuclear weapons capabilities to demonstrate that it is a world power and as such deserves a seat on the United Nations Security Council. If America accedes to India's demand for a seat, however, it could encourage other developing nations to develop a nuclear arsenal as well, the authors argue.

As you read, consider the following questions:

1. As stated by the authors, why does the United States disagree with India's claim that China poses a serious threat to India?
2. According to the authors, how often did India side with America on United Nations votes in 1999?

Larry M. Wortzel and Dana R. Dillon, "U.S. Foreign Policy Towards India Should Not Compromise U.S. Security," www.capitalismmagazine.com, January 4, 2001. Copyright © 2001 by Larry M. Wortzel. Reproduced by permission.

America and India share the distinction of being the world's largest "democracies." Yet relations between the two countries have been unsteady and will need executive attention if they are to improve. A major stumbling block to relations in recent years has been India's testing of nuclear weapons and its missile development program, both of which threaten regional stability.

The United States Should Not Be Swayed

Now, as part of a program to accelerate economic modernization, India is seeking U.S. assistance to develop its commercial satellite and space launch capabilities. Although helping India to improve its economy and increasing opportunities for U.S. businesses in India are good foreign policy objectives, history has shown that there are limits to how far the United States should go in transferring sensitive technology that could be used in weapons development or ballistic missile programs. Washington should not be swayed, either by rhetoric about India's democracy and its new nuclear power status or by suggestions of increased trade, into placing India's interests before U.S. national security concerns.

During a visit to Washington in 2000, Indian Prime Minister Atal Behari Vajpayee spoke before the U.S.-India Business Summit, recognizing that "The United States is today India's largest trading partner. The US companies are also the largest investors in India. . . . We would like to deepen this relationship." Building on this theme when he addressed a joint session of Congress, Vajpayee said that "In the years ahead, a strong, democratic and economically prosperous India, standing at the crossroads of all the major cultural and economic zones of Asia, will be an indispensable factor of stability in the region." Indian officials have asked for greater cooperation in the field of satellite technology and space launches. Inherent in these remarks is India's desire to be seen today as strategically important to the United States. . . .

India's Security Concerns

Historically, however, U.S.-India trade relations have long been overshadowed by the two countries' political and security differences. During the Cold War, relations were inhibited by India's pursuit of nonalignment and by U.S. regional security goals that led it to pursue close relations with Pakistan. Neither side perceived a benefit in developing closer economic relations; during periods of political or security tension, programs to aid commerce were either halted or delayed.

After the Cold War, a new interest in economic development led New Delhi to seek better relations with Washington and Washington to reassess its relations with Pakistan in favor of India. But when India detonated five nuclear weapons in May 1998, Washington reimposed economic sanctions, and mutual mistrust has generally guided engagement since then. Though most of the restrictions have now been lifted, the grave concerns that continue to surround India's efforts to gain nuclear weapons and ballistic missile capabilities make the issue of helping India develop space launch and satellite capabilities more problematic.

India claims that its nuclear and missile development programs are in part a response to the growing security threat it perceives from China—an assessment not fully shared by Washington. The United States believes that Beijing has greater territorial concerns, such as Taiwan, the South China Sea, and "American hegemony" in Asia, than border disputes with India. Indeed, the border disputes that led to the Sino-Indian war in 1962 are the subject of continuing negotiations, and armed separatist movements in Tibet have not received India's support for many years. Nevertheless, India's concerns about China's potential threat cannot be simply dismissed. . . .

The Risk of Misused Technology

India's effort to gain U.S. assistance in developing its satellite and space launch capabilities ostensibly is meant to help bring India into the 21st century in telecommunications and commercial enterprise. However, such technologies could be used to advance India's strategic missile programs. Privately, in fact, Indian officials have indicated that New Delhi hopes to develop thermonuclear weapons, multiple independently targeted reentry vehicles (MIRVs), and intercontinental ballistic missiles (ICBMs). Moreover, some of these officials have argued that India needs a "360 degree" deterrent, suggesting that its future missile programs could target regions other than China.

Such defense imperatives present a significant dilemma for the United States, which believes in helping developing countries to improve their economies. But the technologies used in commercial satellite and space launches could aid India's strategic missile programs. Weather satellites could provide data to ensure that ICBMs are properly aimed, while other satellites could facilitate targeting. . . .

India's Campaign for Recognition

India is hoping that the United States will support its efforts to gain a permanent seat on the U.N. Security Council. One motivation for seeking permanent membership in the Security Council is India's rivalry with China. New Delhi has argued that the two countries are the most populous in the world; thus, Indian membership in the Security Council is only proper. China's permanent seat on the council makes China more powerful diplomatically than India. New Delhi, on the other hand, is nearly invisible, or at least the most populous state among many "equals" in the General Assembly, though occasionally it is able to occupy a temporary seat on the Security Council.

The Security Council is indisputably the U.N.'s premier political body. Nearly every important U.N. decision must originate in or be approved by the Security Council. The council nominates the candidates for membership in the General Assembly and for Secretary General. It also is the only body that can initiate U.N. peacekeeping missions and impose economic sanctions.

Expanding the number of members on the Security Council is not in the best interests of the United States. Adding new permanent members would increase the complexity and difficulty of negotiating resolutions and thereby reduce the Security Council's effectiveness. Gridlock in the Security Council would be of little benefit to the United States or to India.

Certainly, other countries have strong arguments for obtaining a permanent seat on the council. Japan and Germany, for example, are major contributors to the U.N. budgets. Japan contributes $216 million annually and Germany contributes $104 million, compared with India's annual $350,000. Both Japan and Germany are developed countries and economic powers; India is neither. In pursuing nuclear capabilities, India hopes to demonstrate that, despite its economic problems, it is a major world power and deserves a seat on the council. But acceding to its demands could encourage other developing nations to pursue nuclear capabilities as well, if only to use them as leverage in the United Nations.

Finally, the United States has little reason to expect India to side with its positions in the Security Council if it were to become a permanent member. India, which takes pride in its traditional independent stance, sided with the United States on U.N. votes in 1999 less than 22 percent of the time. The Russian Federation, by comparison, voted with the United States 46 percent of the time. Among Asian nations, only China, Laos, Vietnam, Burma, and North Korea voted with the United States fewer times than did India. A 1997 analysis of U.N. votes showed that India—the fifth highest recipient of U.S. aid in FY 1997—had voted against the United States at the U.N. an astounding 80 percent of the time, more than any of the top 10 aid recipients. . . .

Establishing New U.S.-India Relations

The Prime Minister's visit to Washington should be seen as a genuine attempt by both countries to improve relations, which seemed to bend with every political wind. Despite their differences, a closer relationship is in both countries' long-term interests. The United States and India must begin to view themselves as friendly countries that have complementary, though not identical, goals.

To move U.S. policy in this direction, the U.S. government should:

Explain to India that accelerating its nuclear weapons programs is in neither India's nor America's best interests. Indian leaders believe that being a nuclear power makes India a major international actor that deserves a strategic partnership with the United States. While it may not be possible to reverse India's nuclear and missile developments, there are specific steps Washington can take to limit India's nuclear activities. The United States should emphasize, for example, that reducing nuclear weapons and adhering to the Nuclear Nonproliferation Treaty are better guarantees of security than developing a nuclear deterrent and provoking an arms race. It should encourage strategic dialogue between India and China on limiting their nuclear weapons and aggressively pursue discussions on proliferation with India, China, and Russia to confine the spread of nuclear weapons. Moreover, the United States should make clear that a naval arms race to gain regional control of sea lanes—which could interrupt the free flow of goods through the area—would be in no one's best interests.

The United States Could Become India's Target

As things stand, the U.S. threat [to India] is usually portrayed as subsidiary and remote, one that it is politically incorrect to talk about openly. Nevertheless, with time, as India's missile and submarine programs go forward, we should expect to see far more open references to the American threat. With long-range [nuclear] missile capability, it will be technically feasible to mount a retaliatory strike against the continental United States. If it becomes technically possible to do so, there will undoubtedly be those who will push to make it operationally viable.

Kanti Bajpai, *Dissent*, Fall 2001.

Avoid technology cooperation that could improve India's ballistic missile programs. The experience with China in the transfer of sensitive technology should provide ample lessons that commercial space launch and satellite business can be used to advance missile programs. The Administration should consider the recommendations of the Cox Committee, which tend toward limiting U.S. assistance to India's satellite and space launch sector, and develop policies to ensure that commercial activity with India in the satellite and space launch sectors takes place within the same parameters that the United States has imposed on Russia and China.

Encourage and assist India in adhering to World Trade Organization (WTO) standards. Trade is easily the most neglected facet of the U.S.-India relationship. Although domestic political forces in both countries are opposed to trade and globalization in general, developing the relationship between the United States and India has attracted broad support. Opening up its economy and increasing two-way commerce will enhance India's reliability as a democratic partner enormously. However, India continues to claim developing country status and to demand special exemptions from the WTO agreement. At the WTO ministerial meeting in Seattle, for example, New Delhi criticized the high cost of implementing WTO measures. Admittedly, some elements of the agreement, such as protection of property rights and customs regulations, have a price tag that could be high for an economy of India's size. But the cost of not implementing the agreement is lost trade opportunities and cautious foreign investment. The United States should assure India that investing in its own future is vital and that the WTO agreement provides the best way to do so. It should demonstrate to India that improving bilateral trade is among its policy priorities and that transitory political crises will not be allowed to affect those relations.

Refrain from getting involved in internecine territorial disputes between competing regional powers, such as between India and China or between India and Pakistan over Kashmir. The United States has little role in resolving the conflicts over the Northeast Frontier Area and the Aksai-Chin, territories over which both India and China claim sovereignty. Pakistan's long-brewing hostility toward India dates back to the creation of these countries as separate states in 1947. Pakistan continues to be ruled by a military dictatorship that is troubled by a rapidly unraveling economy, while India is evolving as a stable and strong democracy with a reforming economy. Yet there is no American advantage in taking sides in their conflict over Kashmir. Correct and sincere neutrality will benefit the situation as well as U.S. interests.

Explain that giving India a permanent seat on the United Nations Security Council is not in America's best interests at this time. Given the current makeup of the Security Council, India's accession appears highly unlikely. Therefore, consulting with India on matters of mutual interest in the long term may bring India into a closer strategic alignment with the United States and convince its next generation of leaders to view cooperation with America as more important to its future stability and relations than the appearance of independence.

Preparing for the Future

India has clearly demonstrated its interest in developing a closer relationship with the United States. Washington should take this opportunity to foster a meaningful strategic dialogue with Indian officials about U.S. concerns, such as proliferation, and to find ways to limit mischief by China and Russia in the region. Such an approach could result in better cooperation in both trade and security in the future.

"Concerned governments should enact and/or enforce legislation to abolish caste-based discrimination."

The International Community Should Condemn India's Caste System

Human Rights Watch

Human Rights Watch (HRW) is an international organization that works to protect human rights worldwide. In the following viewpoint, the organization urges the international community to enact laws against India's caste system. According to HRW, Dalits—Indians who occupy the bottom of India's rigid caste system—are routinely denied basic human rights. The organization claims that Dalits may not use the same wells, visit the same temples and churches, or drink from the same cups in tea stalls as Indians who occupy higher castes. Moreover, rape, murder, and arson against Dalits are commonplace, the organization claims.

As you read, consider the following questions:
1. In what other Asian countries is caste-based abuse prevalent, as cited by Human Rights Watch?
2. According to HRW, how many people in India are bonded laborers?
3. Why has violence against Dalits increased since the early 1990s, as stated by the organization?

More than 240 million people in South Asia live a precarious existence, shunned by much of society because of their ranks as untouchables or Dalits at the bottom of a rigid caste system. Dalits are discriminated against, denied access to land, forced to work in slave-like conditions, and routinely abused, even killed, at the hands of the police and of higher-caste groups that enjoy the state's protection.

Dalits in India may not cross the line dividing their part of the village from that occupied by higher castes. They may not use the same wells, visit the same temples and churches, drink from the same cups in tea stalls, or lay claim to land that is legally theirs. Dalit children are frequently made to sit in the back of classrooms, and communities as a whole are made to perform degrading rituals in the name of caste. Dalit women are frequent victims of sexual abuse.

In what has been called Asia's hidden apartheid, entire villages in many Indian states remain completely segregated by caste. Caste-based abuse is also prevalent in Nepal, Sri Lanka, Bangladesh, Pakistan, Japan, and several African states.

The Situation

Over 100,000 cases of rape, murder, arson, and other atrocities against Dalits are reported in India each year. Given that Dalits are both reluctant and unable (for lack of police cooperation) to report crimes against themselves, the actual number of abuses is presumably much higher.

India's own agencies have reported that these cases are typically related to attempts by Dalits to defy the social order, or demand minimum wages and their basic human rights. Many of the atrocities are committed by the police. Even perpetrators of large-scale massacres have escaped prosecution.

An estimated forty million people in India, among them fifteen million children, are bonded laborers, working in slave-like conditions in order to pay off a debt. A majority of them are Dalits.

According to government statistics, an estimated one million Dalits are manual scavengers who clear feces from public and private latrines and dispose of dead animals; unofficial estimates are much higher.

The sexual slavery of Dalit girls and women continues to

The Indian Caste System

According to the Hindu law-giver Manu, every Indian is born into one of four principle Varnas, or large categories, and must remain within that caste until death. Dalits are not considered worthy to be included in the Varna system.

Brahmins	Kshatriyas	Vaishyas	Shudras	"Untouchables," including Dalits
Priests and teachers, presiding over knowledge and education	Rulers and soldiers	Merchants and traders	Peasants, laborers, and artisans	Assigned tasks too "ritually polluting" to merit inclusion with the traditional Varna system

Information obtained from Gopal Guru and Shiraz Sidhva, *Unesco Courier*, September 2001.

receive religious sanction. Under the devadasi system, thousands of Dalit girls in India's southern states are ceremoniously dedicated or married to a deity or to a temple. Once dedicated, they are unable to marry, forced to become prostitutes for upper-caste community members, and eventually auctioned into an urban brothel.

Developments

Since the early 1990s, violence against Dalits has escalated dramatically in response to a growing Dalit rights movement.

Although untouchability was abolished under India's constitution in 1950, and numerous laws have since been enacted to tackle caste-related problems of bonded labor, manual scavenging, devadasi [forced temple prostitution], and other atrocities against Dalit community members, much of the legislation remains completely unenforced. Laws are openly flouted and state complicity in attacks on Dalit communities has become a well-documented pattern.

In December 1999, the National Campaign for Dalit Human Rights—a grassroots movement of Indian human rights groups in fourteen states—collectively submitted over 2.5 million signatures to the Indian prime minister demanding the abolishment of untouchability and urging U.N. bodies to squarely address the issue of caste-based abuse and discrimination.

Numerous U.N. treaty bodies have called on the Indian government to improve the situation of Dalits. The United Nations Committee on the Elimination of All Forms of Racial Discrimination (CERD) has clearly stated that the situation of Dalits falls within the scope of the Convention on the Elimination of All Forms of Racial Discrimination, and that the term descent contained in Article 1 of the Convention does not refer solely to race, and encompasses the situation of Dalits.

Activists from around the world, including anti-apartheid activists in South Africa and African-American activists in the United States, have already begun to support the Dalit struggle.

The Indian government has consistently attempted to sabotage the efforts of Indian nongovernment organizations (NGOs) to raise awareness of the caste struggle at preparatory meetings in the lead-up to the World Conference on Racism (WCAR). The situation of Dalits stands alone as the only issue to have been systematically cut out of the conference's intergovernmental process so far.

Next Steps

India and other concerned governments should enact and/or enforce legislation to abolish caste-based discrimination, and where applicable, caste-related practices of untouchability, bonded labor, manual scavenging, and the devadasi system.

Concerned governments should also extend invitations to the Special Rapporteur on racism to investigate caste-based discrimination and other forms of discrimination based on descent in their respective countries.

All nations should ensure that caste-based and similar discrimination against marginalized populations in Asia and Africa is explicitly addressed in the draft declaration and programme of action of the WCAR.

Dalits, Burakumin in Japan, and other populations in similar situations should be explicitly acknowledged as groups of people who have been subject to perennial and persistent forms of discrimination and abuse on the basis of their descent.

> *"India's dalits indeed face all manner of deprivations and discrimination within India. But India as a nation also remains deeply deprived and discriminated by the so-called 'world community.'"*

The International Community Is in No Position to Condemn India's Caste System

Shishir Thadani

Shishir Thadani has a postgraduate degree from Yale University and an undergraduate degree from New Delhi. He has written several articles on Indian history and contemporary life. In the following viewpoint, Thadani contends that international condemnation of India's caste system is hypocritical and ineffective. First, the nations critical of India's caste system are those responsible for perpetuating it during India's occupation by imperial powers. Second, Thadani argues, if concerned nations really wanted to help the Indian people, they would encourage the poorest Indians to immigrate to their nations where they could make better lives for themselves.

As you read, consider the following questions:

1. According to Thadani, where does caste discrimination tend to be most egregious?
2. What kinds of Indians are other nations most likely to accept as immigrants, as stated by Thadani?
3. As cited by the author, what was India's share of manufactured output in 1750?

B oth the Indian and the international media have paid
considerable attention to the debate on whether caste
discrimination is also a form of racism. As the controversy
rages within India, one of the most important questions that
should be asked is—what are the real solutions? How can international conferences or UN agencies or the so-called
"World Community" of nations help India's most discriminated and oppressed communities?

Hyprocrisy and Sanctimoniousness

And this is where the utter hypocrisy and sanctimoniousness
of the so-called "international community" lies exposed. As
should be well-known to most objective students of world
history, social discrimination and oppression were not
unique to any one nation. Even those unfamiliar with European history, but with just a fleeting acquaintance with authors such as Charles Dickens, would know that the treatment of the poor and unschooled was quite abominable just
a few centuries ago.

As the European nations colonized the rest of the world,
and displaced the native American communities from their
native lands, the internal contradictions amongst the European nations receded—and did so quite dramatically. Thus,
in these newly conquered territories, White European
racism became the primary cause of social oppression in society. Amongst the nations that were at the receiving end of
colonization (such as India), older forms of discrimination
became aggravated. The economic devastation that followed
colonial rule led to the further ossification of caste divisions.

But how much of the discussion on the problems of caste
in India acknowledges this crucial and essential aspect of the
problem? Is there any real attempt at addressing the colossal
crime that was colonial rule and exploitation? Are the world's
former colonial powers willing to pay compensation to those
who suffered most? How about a fund that would pay for the
education, housing and healthcare of those in India living below the poverty line? How about free access to technologies
and capital that could assist India in solving its perennial water and power shortages? How about the oil-rich nations
(who use hundreds of thousands of Indian workers to pump

their oil) helping out by providing subsidies to India for buying oil (at least at cost, if not at a discount)?

In fact, there are many concrete ways in which the international community could help. Even a cursory look at where caste discrimination in India is most egregious will show that caste discrimination tends to be greater in areas of the country that are very densely populated and relatively less urbanized and industrialized. Wherever the economy is stagnant, social problems are aggravated. Thus, problems of caste discrimination are greatest in states like Bihar (pop. density 880 per sq. km), UP (689) and Tamil Nadu (478). Compare these to Australia (2), Brazil (20), US (30), South Africa (36), Turkey (85), or Italy (193).

Although the so-called "international community" has been very aggressive in calling for the "free" movement of capital—there is deep resistance to allowing for the free movement of labour. Whereas India's best educated are now permitted to migrate to nations such as the US, Canada, Australia and New Zealand, and even some of the European nations are issuing temporary work visas for highly educated and skilled workers, no one is willing to even consider issuing immigrant visas to India's poor—to the unschooled or poorly schooled.

No Official Apartheid

India does not practise anything like official apartheid. On the contrary, a fifth of the seats in Parliament are reserved for members of scheduled castes and tribes [or the "Untouchables," including the Dalit]. They and other lower castes have places at educational institutions and jobs in government ear-marked for them. Some states have powerful political parties based on alliances among lower castes.

Economist, June 16, 2001.

Nations particularly perturbed about India's caste problems could provide a very simple solution. Allow the migration of India's dalits, offer them jobs, or adult education classes for a year or two, and allow them to integrate with dignity into their societies. Instead of drawing away India's best educated, accept India's weakest citizens. Even other developing nations could make such an offer, especially since the vast majority of them are much less densely populated when compared to India.

But the truth is that no one who bemoans India's caste problems wants to actually lend a helping hand. Rich industrialized nations that accept India's well-educated are far less open when it comes to accepting less-qualified relatives, and even spouses can face lengthy processing delays. The oil-rich nations of the Middle East exploit India's poor to the hilt, yet they are not even willing to offer Indian Muslims (let alone other Indians) permanent visas or any form of protection from discrimination or exploitation. There are virtually no rights for workers or workers compensation schemes for even the most blatant forms of social discrimination or ill-treatment.

Discrimination by the World Community

India's dalits indeed face all manner of deprivations and discrimination within India. But India as a nation also remains deeply deprived and discriminated by the so-called "world community". One cannot solve one without solving the other. A lot of sociologists and intellectuals from nations more fortunate than India can feel superior that they don't have such problems—but if they really cared to solve the problems, they would be spending less time making pompous speeches and passing meaningless resolutions.

For centuries, when India was a relatively prosperous and advanced nation (in 1750, India's share of manufactured output was 25%), India welcomed immigrants and the oppressed from many countries, allowed them to form settlements, and permitted them to follow their own customs and religious beliefs. Syrian Christians, Persian Zorastrians, Arab Muslims and Jews, Armenians, Central Asians, Afghans—a host of nationalities and peoples migrated to India. Even those who came as conquerors and invaders were eventually absorbed into the Indian mosaic of ethnic, religious and cultural diversity.

Those in the so-called "international community" who wish to "teach" India how to solve its internal problems might instead do better to learn a bit from India's generous history and reciprocate in kind, through concrete and practical measures, rather than pass smug judgments about India's social "backwardness".

Periodical Bibliography

The following articles have been selected to supplement the diverse views presented in this chapter.

Anne Applebaum — "The New Delhi Order," Slate.com, December 28, 2001. http://slate.msn.com.

Mohammed Ayoob — "India Matters," *Washington Quarterly*, Winter 2000.

H. Sterling Burnett and Wess Mitchell — "India and Us," *National Review*, December 12, 2001.

Economist — "Still Untouchable: Caste in India," June 16, 2001.

Global Agenda — "America's Precarious Ally," September 19, 2001.

Gopal Guru and Shiraz Sidhva — "India's 'Hidden Apartheid,'" *Unesco Courier*, September 2001.

William R. Hawkins — "Wrong Way to Tilt?" *Washington Times*, January 10, 2002.

Michael Krepon — "The Current Crisis in South Asia," Henry Stimson Center, June 6, 2002. www.stimson.org.

Anatol Lieven — "The Pressures on Pakistan," *Foreign Affairs*, January/February 2002.

Nadeem Malik — "Into the Lion's Den in Pakistan," Asia Times Online, May 14, 2002. www.atimes.com.

Scott D. Sagan — "If Pakistan Fell, U.S. Would Face Far Worse Danger," *San Jose Mercury News*, October 14, 2002.

Philip Smucker — "Al Queda Thriving in Pakistani Kashmir," *Christian Science Monitor*, July 2, 2002.

Marin J. Strmecki — "Our Ally, Our Problem: Pakistan Is an Exceptionally Hard Case—Here's What to Do," *National Review*, July 1, 2002.

Ray Takeyh and Nikolas K. Gvosdev — "Rein in Pakistan or Lose India," *Los Angeles Times*, May 24, 2002.

CHAPTER 4

What Lies in the Future for India and Pakistan?

Chapter Preface

In assessing what lies in the future for Pakistan and India, the role that the leading religion plays in each country—Islam in Pakistan, Hinduism in India—cannot be overlooked. In both nations, competing moderate and extremist religious views have been a wellspring of controversy and have fueled debates about what place religion should have in each nation's political institutions.

Islam has been a fundamental part of Pakistan's identity since before the nation's founding in 1947. Pakistan was established as a country where Muslims, who constitute 97 percent of its population, could exist independently of Hindu-dominated India. Islam gained further official influence under General Mohammad Zia-ul-Haq, the military ruler of Pakistan from 1977 to 1988. Zia sought popular support and legitimacy by embracing Islam as the basis of Pakistan's laws, installing devout Muslims in key military posts, and supporting the development of *madrassas*—religious schools taught by Muslim clerics. One result of these developments has been a growing gulf between moderate and fundamentalist followers of Islam. While many Pakistanis, especially in the middle class, favor a secular state and a moderate form of Islam, growing numbers of others (including members of the powerful military) are calling for a theocratic Islamic state similar to Afghanistan under the Taliban. Religious conflicts have resulted in violence between different sects of Islam as well as attacks on Pakistan's Christian minority. Pakistan's current military ruler, General Pervez Musharraf, has criticized Islamic fundamentalists and has ordered the closing of some of Pakistan's extremist *madrassas* and other Islamic organizations, but questions remain as to how far he can go in acting against such movements while still remaining in power.

In India, Hinduism, not Islam, is the leading religion. But while India's population is more than 80 percent Hindu, that means, in a country of over a billion people, that it must also accommodate 150 million Muslims as well as millions of followers of other faiths, including Sikhism and Christianity. The Indian National Congress, which evolved into the Congress Party and dominated Indian politics for decades after independence, was led by Jawaharlal Nehru (India's first prime minister) and others who believed that India should have a secular government with constitutional protections for all religions. Those who called for an official Hindu state found themselves discredited after the assassination of revered independence leader Mahatma Gandhi by a Hindu nationalist in 1948.

In recent years, however, Hindu fundamentalist and nationalist movements have grown in power and influence. The Bharatiya Janata Party, which includes many advocates of a "Hindu rashtra" or Hindu nation, became India's leading parliamentary party in 1998. Intolerance of Muslims and other non-Hindus has grown as well. In 1992 in the city of Ayodhya, a Hindu mob destroyed a mosque (a Muslim place of worship) that was situated on a site where the Hindu god Lord Ram was supposed to have been born (plans have since been made to construct an enormous Hindu temple on the site, further antagonizing Muslims). The incident set off riots throughout India that killed thousands. In the spring of 2002 in the Indian state of Gujarat, religious tensions resulted in the deaths of hundreds of Indians, both Hindu and Muslim, and the destruction of thousands of buildings by mob actions. Some observers in India fear that such violence is inevitable as long as revivalist Hindus preach that Muslims and other non-Hindus are foreigners not to be trusted.

Whether religious conflict will be a defining feature of the future of India and Pakistan remains to be seen. The viewpoints in this chapter examine this and other questions concerning the future of these two nations.

"Reaching one billion [in population] is not a cause for celebration in a country where one half of the adults are illiterate . . . and one third of the people live below the poverty line."

India's Future Is Bleak

Lester R. Brown and Brian Halweil

Sometime around 1999 or 2000, India's population passed the one billion mark (the United Nations designated August 15, 1999—the fifty-second anniversary of India's independence from Great Britain—as the day of this milestone). In the following viewpoint, Lester R. Brown and Brian Halwcil argue that surpassing one billion people is no reason for India to celebrate. Such population growth exacerbates several serious problems India faces, including poverty, illiteracy, and natural resource depletion. Because India's government chose to spend resources for military purposes rather than education and family planning, the nation faces severe problems in its future, they conclude. Brown is the founder and former president of the Worldwatch Institute, an environmental policy research organization. Brian Halweil is a Worldwatch research associate.

As you read, consider the following questions:
1. What is India's population projected to be in 2050, according to Brown and Halweil?
2. What environmental factors threaten India's food supply, according to the authors?
3. How do farm sizes affect population trends in India, according to Brown and Halweil?

Lester R. Brown and Brian Halweil, "India Reaching 1 Billion on August 15: No Celebration Planned," *Worldwatch News Brief*, August 10, 1999. Copyright © 1999 by Worldwatch Institute. Reproduced by permission.

Sometime on Sunday, August 15, 1999, India's population [passed] the one billion mark, making it the second member of the exclusive one billion club, along with China. But reaching one billion is not a cause for celebration in a country where one half of the adults are illiterate, more than half of all children are undernourished, and one third of the people live below the poverty line.

Each year India is adding 18 million people, roughly another Australia. By 2050, U.N. demographers project that it will have added another 530 million people for a total of more than 1.5 billion. If India continues on the demographic path as projected, it will overtake China by 2045, becoming the world's most populous country. Well before hitting the one billion mark, the demands of India's population were outrunning its natural resource base. This can be seen in its shrinking forests, deteriorating rangelands, and falling water tables. For Americans to understand the pressure of population on resources in India, it would be necessary to squeeze the entire U.S. population east of the Mississippi River and then multiply it by four.

Food Shortages

Although India has tripled its grain harvest over the last half century, food production has barely kept up with population. Riceland productivity has doubled while that of wheat has more than tripled. Earlier maturing, high-yield wheats and rices, combined with a tripling of irrigated area, have enabled farmers to double crop winter wheat and summer rice in the north and to double crop rice in the south.

As the nineties unfold, the rise in grainland productivity in India is slowing as it is in many other countries. Against this backdrop, the continuing shrinkage of cropland per person now threatens India's food security. In 1960, each Indian had an average of 0.21 hectares of grainland. By 1999, the average had dropped to 0.10 hectares per person, or less than half as much. And by 2050, it is projected to shrink to a meager 0.07 hectares per person. At this point, an Indian family of five will have to produce their wheat or rice on 0.35 hectares of land or less than one acre—the size of a building lot in a middle class U.S. suburb.

Falling water tables are now also threatening India's food production. The International Water Management Institute (IWMI) estimates that withdrawals of underground water are double the rate of aquifer recharge. As a result, water tables are falling almost everywhere. If pumping of water is double the recharge of an aquifer, then eventual depletion of the aquifer will reduce water pumped by half.

In a country where irrigated land accounts for 55 percent of the grain harvest and where the lion's share of irrigation water comes from underground, falling water tables are generating concern. The IWMI estimates that aquifer depletion could reduce India's grain harvest by one fourth. Falling water tables will likely lead to rising grain prices on a scale that could destabilize not only grain markets, but possibly the government itself. With 53 percent of all children already undernourished and underweight, any drop in food supply can quickly become life threatening.

Education Challenges

With a staggering 338 million children under 15 years of age, India is also facing a major challenge on the educational front. Despite efforts to educate its people during the 52 years since it achieved independence in 1947, some 54 percent of adults in the world's largest democracy cannot read or write. Failure to provide adequate education has undermined efforts to slow population growth since female access to education is a key to smaller families.

Providing enough jobs for the 10 million new entrants into the job market each year is even more difficult. Nowhere is this more evident than in agriculture where the number of farms increased from 48 million in 1960 to 105 million in 1990. Meanwhile, the average farm shrank from 2.7 hectares to less than 1.6 hectares, a reduction of some 42 percent. By 2020, the land will pass to another generation—and another round of fragmentation will occur, shrinking farm size even more, threatening the ability of those living on the land to earn a livelihood, and triggering a potential migration from the land that could inundate India's cities.

After several decades of rapid population growth, the government of India, overwhelmed by sheer numbers, is suffering from demographic fatigue. After trying to educate all the children coming of school age, trying to find jobs for all the young people coming into the job market, and trying to deal with the environmental fallout of rapid population growth, such as deforestation and soil erosion, India's leaders are worn down and its fiscal resources spread thin. As a result, when a new threat emerges, such as aquifer depletion, the government is not able to respond effectively. If this decrease in water supplies causes food production to drop, death rates may start to rise.

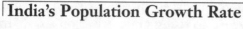

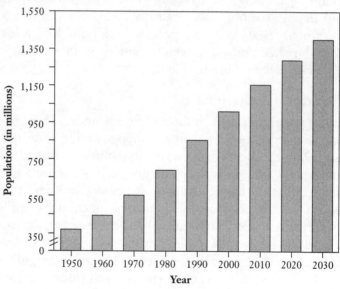

India's Population Growth Rate

Colorado State University.

As noted earlier, India's population is projected to reach 1.5 billion by 2050, but there are doubts as to whether the natural resource base will support such growth. These projections will not materialize either because India accelerates the shift to smaller families, alleviating the projected additional stress on the resource base by reducing births, or because it fails to do so and the combination of deteriorating conditions pushes up death rates.

The prospect of rising death rates as a result of aquifer depletion is no longer as hypothetical as it once seemed. Death rates are already rising in Africa, where governments, also overwhelmed by several decades of rapid population growth, have been unable to respond effectively to the HIV epidemic. As a result, adult infection rates already exceed 20 percent in several countries, including Botswana, South Africa, and Zimbabwe. In the absence of a medical breakthrough, these countries will likely lose one fifth of their adult population within the next decade. In Zimbabwe, a model of development in Africa until a few years ago, life expectancy has fallen from 60 years in 1990 to 44 years at present and is expected to drop to 39 years by 2010.

Priorities Must Change

In some ways, India today is paying the price for its earlier indiscretions when, despite its impoverished state, it invested in a costly effort to design and produce nuclear weapons and succeeded in becoming a member of the nuclear club. As a result, it now has a nuclear arsenal capable of protecting the largest concentration of impoverished citizens on earth.

Even today, India spends 2.5 percent of its GNP for military purposes but only 0.7 percent on health, which includes family planning. Unless India can quickly reorder priorities, it risks falling into a demographic dark hole, one where population will begin to slow because death rates are rising.

It may be time for India to redefine security. The principal threat now may not be military aggression from without but population growth from within.

"In the case of India, the achievement of the whole is greater than the sum of its flawed parts."

India's Future Is Bright

Prasenjit Basu

Prasenjit Basu is an economist at Credit Suisse First Boston in Singapore. In the following viewpoint, he argues that India has achieved remarkable results in lifting its people out of poverty while creating and maintaining a democratic system of government. India's economic growth and rising literacy rates constitute an untold success story that bodes well for India's future, he concludes.

As you read, consider the following questions:
1. Why did India lag behind South Korea and Taiwan in economic growth and literacy rates, according to Basu?
2. What historically unprecedented task is India attempting, according to the author?
3. What future prediction does Basu make about India?

Prasenjit Basu, "Take a Better Look at the Work of a Rebounding India," *International Herald Tribune*, August 20, 1999. Copyright © 1999 by New York Times Syndicate. Reproduced by permission.

India recently passed two milestones: the 52nd anniversary of its independence [August 15, 1999] and, by some estimates, the birth of its billionth living citizen. The latter event was accompanied by a lecture from Lester R. Brown and Brian Halweil ... about the need to spend on health care and primary education rather than on defense.

A Growing Economy

Virtually unremarked on Independence Day ... was the fact that India's real gross domestic product (GDP) has sustained a compound annual growth rate of 6.5 percent for the last six years [1993–1999]—a performance that makes its economy the fastest growing among the world's democracies.

Indian software exports have increased at an annual rate of 65 percent over the same period, and agricultural production by 4 percent—well ahead of the 1.8 percent pace of population growth. Food grain output has trebled in the last 30 years.

It is also worth celebrating what India is not. It is not seeking handouts from the rest of the world. (Net inflows of foreign aid amount to considerably less than $1 per person.) Nor is it among the 42 highly indebted poor countries for which debt forgiveness is now being worked out. In fact, India has never had to undertake a rescheduling of its external debt.

Education and Literacy

During 190 years of British colonial rule, India was regularly afflicted by famine. Since independence it has had none. And despite some serious religious and ethnic conflict, India has remained united.

In 1947, India inherited an economy that had grown at an annual pace of 0.7 percent in the previous 50 years, less than the rate of population increase. It had an adult literacy rate of 14 percent and a higher education system oriented toward producing a narrow elite of imperial bureaucrats.

By contrast, South Korea and Taiwan at that time had adult literacy rates in excess of 50 percent (a level that India achieved only at the beginning of the 1990s). They had, after all, been ruled by a country, Japan, which was the first after the United States to achieve universal literacy, and so paid special attention to education. That difference in the initial endowment of human capital (plus massive infusions of external aid per capita in the early years) goes most of the way toward explaining the faster trajectory of their initial growth.

But India can and must do better. The untapped potential remains enormous, especially when you consider the talents and achievements of India's diaspora in business, technology and the professions.

India's Bright Spots

There are surely some bright spots in India. It is still the largest parliamentary democracy in the world. Moreover, since 1991 large-scale capital has been invested in India, and a new software computer industry has developed in Mumbai [Bombay], Hyderabad, Bangalore, and elsewhere. This is due in large part to the removal of burdensome governmental regulations and the opening up of a free market for foreign capital. Indian computer specialists are now regarded among the best in the world. As a result of this and other industrial developments, a growing middle class of some 250 million people is emerging.

Paul Kurtz, *Free Inquiry*, Spring 1999.

For approximately 200 years, India has had a larger number of illiterate and poorly nourished people than any other country on the planet. Presumably it was not always so. According to the Yale historian Paul Kennedy, India accounted for about 24.5 percent of world manufacturing output in 1750, a share that fell to 1.7 percent by 1900 as the per capita level of industrialization declined sevenfold.

A Successful Democracy

Never before in human history has there been an attempt to lift a population of even 150 million, let alone 400 million, out of abject poverty within a democratic system. India is making that valiant attempt and, ever so gradually, beginning to succeed.

The point is that in the case of India, the achievement of the whole is greater than the sum of its flawed parts. Despite stresses, its society remains secular. Its prime minister may be a Hindu, but the creator of its nuclear bomb and its richest entrepreneur are Muslims, the creator of its recent economic miracle is a Sikh, and its defense minister is a Christian.

India's judiciary is lumbering and slow, but it maintains a genuine check on both the legislature and the executive. Parliament appears chaotic, but it unfailingly produces laws that are humane and faithful to the country's secular tradition. The executive is overstaffed and almost always poorly led, but it can never function arbitrarily because of the checks and balances in the democratic system.

Despite a ponderous state, economic growth has accelerated from the 3.5 percent of the first three decades of independence to 5.5 percent in the 1980s and 6.5 percent in the 1990s. Inflation has rarely reached double digits, while current account deficits have usually been less than 2 percent of GDP. Only on fiscal policy have there been serious slippages in the past two decades. Adult literacy has risen from 52 percent in 1991 to an estimated 65 percent today.

An Untold Success Story

As a democracy with functioning institutions and a vibrant capital market, India has been the great, if largely untold, success story of the 1990s. Where Russia failed, India succeeded in completing a rapid transition away from quasi-socialism. With its vast army of professionals and its abundance of labor at every level of skill and creativity, it can achieve more in the decade ahead.

What remains is for the talents of the vast rural population to be effectively deployed in labor-intensive exports, and for urban infrastructure to improve without further increasing the budget deficit.

Then, perhaps, a decade from now, India will begin to benefit fully from the return of what the late Prime Minister Rajiv Gandhi called its overseas "brain deposit," and become again the economic beacon that once attracted the European explorers Christopher Columbus and Vasco da Gama.

*"Of all the reforms that we did in 1991 in
India, I think the most important one was
to link ourselves with the world."*

Global Capitalism Will Enrich
India

Gurcharan Das

For several decades following independence in 1947, India
pursued socialist-oriented policies in which the state planned
development projects, restricted free trade, and regulated
businesses. Beginning in 1991, however, India has taken several steps to deregulate business and open itself up to foreign
trade and investment. In the following viewpoint, Gurcharan
Das, a business consultant and journalist, argues that such reforms have benefited India by unleashing economic growth
and creating a rapidly growing middle class. Das is a former
corporate executive in charge of Procter & Gamble's Indian
operations; the following consists of remarks made at a forum
discussing his book *India Unbound*.

As you read, consider the following questions:
1. What general economic prediction does Das make at the
   beginning of the viewpoint?
2. What is the "Theorem of Convergence," according to
   the author?
3. What hypotheses does Das give for India's proficiency at
   information technology?

I am going to offer you a proposition, that if I had offered this even 10 years ago you would have thought me a fitting candidate for the nearest lunatic asylum. I am going to suggest we begin by imagining a map of India. I don't know how many of you can picture a map of India. It's basically an upside-down triangle. You connect the north city of Kanpur with Chennai, which is Madras, and one of the theses of my book is that 50 percent of the people west of that line will turn middleclass by 2020. And it will take another 20 years before the same thing will happen east of the line.

Now, why do I talk about the middleclass? Because most people would talk about poverty when it comes to India. I speak in terms of the middleclass because in any given society, in any society, the top 15 to 20 percent will succeed regardless and we don't have to worry about them. The bottom 15 to 20 percent will fail and we need to look after them. But in between is the 60 to 70 percent that, in successful economies, has become the middleclass.

The tragedy of India over the last 50 years is not that we have poor people but that we deliberately suppressed the middleclass for this period. And even as late as 1980, only 8 percent of the people constituted the middleclass. We have a National Council of Applied Economic Research, NCAER, which makes these definitions. They don't really call it the middleclass. They use the words "consuming class," but the idea is the same. I used their numbers. . . .

Even now [in 2001], when the middleclass has more than tripled . . . it is still less than 20 percent of the population. Now, you might say, well, 20 percent of 1 billion, that's 200 million people; that's a large middleclass. Yes, it is. But for the Indian society, it is still a failure until you get to that 50-percent level.

So why do I make this outrageous proposition that India is . . . going to turn middleclass? I have two and a half reasons. . . . And they go back really to two very old ideas in economics. The first idea is an idea that goes back to Adam Smith. And that is the idea that if a rich country and a poor country are linked together by trade or investment, then the standard of living of the two should eventually converge. This is called the Theorem of Convergence.

The idea itself is fairly intuitively straightforward—that if the standard of living depends on productivity, and productivity in turn has so far been linked pretty close to technology, so when a rich and a poor country are linked together the poor country merely takes the technology from the rich country. It doesn't have to reinvent the wheel. The rich country may have taken 50 years, 100 years, to come to that point of technology. And we can see that every day with computers and cell phones that we use in India. They were not invented there but yet they are having a huge impact on productivity for the people who use them.

So the question, though, in your minds, I'm sure, is: But why haven't I seen convergence in the last 50 years? It makes sense that the convergence should take place, but it seems that the rich countries have grown richer and the poor countries, while they may not have grown poorer but they certainly have not converged. And the answer to that question also is fairly simple—that they were not linked in the last 50 years, until recently.

Basically, after the Second World War, you had three kinds of countries. You had what we called the First World, the Second World and the Third World. The First World were the rich Western countries. Now, these countries were linked and we did see convergence take place. Because the poor countries before the Second World War—countries like Italy, Portugal and Spain—were quite poor. And after the War, by the early seventies, the standard of living started to converge, the Southern European countries with the Northern European countries. So convergence took place in the First World.

The Second World, of course, was the communist world. That was closed. So let's move to the Third World.

The Third World

Jeff Sachs and Andrew Warner [Harvard University economists] did a study which was published in the Brookings Institution papers in January of 1995 . . . where they examined 87 countries. And in these 87 countries they found that 74 of these 87 were closed. Only 13 were open. That means they were linked with the global economy.

The 13 that were open grew six times faster than the 74 that were closed. This was a study done between 1965 and 1990, so 25 years. Over that 25-year period, the 13 open economies outperformed the others by six times. And can you guess where those 13 virtuous countries were? Most of them were in the Far East. So, in fact, convergence did take place certainly for those 13 virtuous countries.

The difference, though, now between the world in 1970 is only 20 percent of the world's population lived in open economies. Today, more than 80 percent of the world lives in open economies. . . .

Of all the reforms that we did in 1991 in India, I think the most important one was to link ourselves with the world. That was where essentially we lowered import barriers, lowered import tariffs, made the currency slowly convertible on the trade account, and really joined up with the global economy. We still have high tariffs compared to many countries, but it is a sea change over what existed.

Growth Rates

And really, the fundamental reason to believe what I said about 2020 and 2040 is the economic reforms that we have done and that we are in the process of making happen. A lot of us get very frustrated at the slow pace of those reforms, but the direction has been pretty much one way, in the right direction, since 1991. And I would say that if you look at the performance of the Indian economy, it is hard to do a one-to-one linkup between growth rates and reforms. But, nevertheless, if we look at a wide enough picture—let's take 100 years, from 1900 to 2000, a big enough time period—. . . between 1900 and 1950, the Indian economy grew around 1 percent, but the population also grew around 1 percent. So the per capita income grew at zero. And that is why we rightly said that our economy had been a stagnant economy in the Colonial period.

After independence, from 1950 to 1980, the economy's rate of growth picked up, to 3.5 percent, but the population also picked up, from 1 percent to 2.2 percent. So, in fact, the net per capita income growth was 3.5 minus 2.2, which is 1.3. And this is what we moaned and groaned was the Hindu rate of growth. Because after doing everything, you still got 1.3. Mind you, India was one of those 74 closed economies, so its growth rate mirrored pretty much the growth rate of the 74 countries.

A Growing Economic Power

India as a whole has successfully overcome its "Hindu rate of growth"—the sardonic term coined by the late Raj Krishna, one of India's most distinguished economists. Under Nehru, the economy grew at a rate of 3.5 percent a year, twice as fast as the 1.3 percent averaged during the first half of the century under the Raj and faster than Britain's own growth rate during its industrial revolution. Over the past five years, growth has hovered around 5 to 6 percent. In 1999, the Indian economy had among the world's fastest growth rates (6 percent). Indians talk confidently of reaching 7 to 8 percent. If the country sustains the pace of its reforms and moves to the next phase, its national income could double in a decade. India's 1998 GNP of $420 billion was the world's eleventh largest; its GNP measured at purchasing power parity was $1,660 billion, the world's fifth largest, behind the United States, China, Japan, and Germany. . . .

The facts of Indian poverty are undeniable and remain both a moral issue and a political embarrassment to any Indian government. Yet the Indian economy continued to expand at 6.1 percent a year between 1990 and 1998. As India's population growth rate levels off, its identity may no longer be overdefined by its poverty. India is likely to surpass Pakistan in per capita income in several years, which will further strengthen its regional position.

Stephen P. Cohen, *India: Emerging Power*, 2001.

Between 1980 and 1990, the growth rate picked up. It picked up to 5.6 percent. And the population growth rate basically stayed pretty much the same at 2.1. But you still got 5.6 minus 2.1, so you have 3.5 percent per capita income growth. Now, that is beginning to move upwards.

And from 1990 to 2000, the last decade, the growth rate has been 6.4 percent per year, and the population, for the first time in decades, has begun to slow down. It's a small slowdown. The average still for the decade was 1.8. But you are talking about a per capita income growth of 4.6. Now, if any of you has a compound interest calculator, you can see that over 10 years of a 4.6 percent growth rate certainly means that the economy is more than 50 percent richer at the end of the decade than it was before.

So here is an economy which . . . has grown at 6 percent average for 20 years. Now, you have to remember that the industrial revolution in the West took place at a growth rate of 3 percent. So, what is going to happen in the future?

From my perspective, the base case would be a 7 percent growth rate and a 1.5 percent population rate, which would be 5.5 percent. And one could be a few points off here, but a 5.5 percent per capita income growth rate for the next three decades is what I would project. . . .

I call it a base case, because really, no matter who is in power, their ability to do harm to the growth rate is somewhat limited—much less than what it was before. So that's why I called [my book] "India Unbound." There has been a liberation from politicians themselves to do this.

Indians and the Information Age

Now, I said two and a half reasons. Very quickly, let me give you the second reason why I think we have this good future. And this future, by the way, it is not India alone, as I said. If India can conquer poverty, I think the whole world can. The second reason has to do with the world's change from an economy that was basically a manufacturing/industrial economy to a knowledge economy. And for some reason Indians are performing well in this services/knowledge economy.

And I explain this reason in my book. I speculate, of course. And this has partly I think to do with our Brahminical heritage. And it is the same Brahminical heritage which came in the way of succeeding in the industrial economy. It came in the way because the Brahmins have contempt for manual labor and they have reverence for knowledge. So that contempt for manual labor, you need tinkerers to create industrial revolutions. And tinkerers need to combine working with hands with knowledge.

And we prevented the people who work with hands from getting knowledge. So what you have, those are the Sudras and the Brahmins. And the Banyas, who are the people who run businesses, they basically are also upper caste. And they have the same values of the Brahmins. They have the same contempt for manual labor.

Anyway, my time is running out, so I am not going to be able to fully explain this. But what I want to say, though, is that what was a negative has become a positive. In other words, the Brahminical heritage, which was a negative from the point of view of the values that it brought to the industrial age now brings a positive value. In other words, that reverence for knowledge is what is helping the country. . . .

A New Green Revolution

The final reason really has to do with I believe India is on the verge of a second green revolution. And like the first green revolution, this is also technology based. And it will be based on the miracle [genetically engineered] seeds. . . . But a green revolution will require a lot of other things. You have to change the agricultural economy from basically a peasant economy. No peasant economy created green revolutions. What creates green revolutions are agribusinesses. . . .

In a sense, the WTO [World Trade Organization] is our best friend in this regard. The WTO will slowly open up the agricultural markets. India has plenty of sunshine, plenty of water, plenty of arable land. We have twice the arable land of China and one-third the productivity. So you can see how far one can go. So, in a sense, if China is going to clothe us, we can feed China and provide China with software. . . .

Let me just close with an anecdote. I left P&G [Procter & Gamble] at the age of 50. I took early retirement and went back to India. There was a friend of Swami's, named Niman, who was editor of *Business World* and *Business Standard*, two respected business newspapers and journals. He said, why don't you go around the country and tell us what has happened to the country after the economic reforms.

And the first trip that I took in that journey was from Madras to Pondicherry. And we stopped in the morning at a roadside cafe. And it was just a village cafe, nothing fancy. It was under the trees. And this boy, Raju, was serving us coffee, good, South Indian coffee. And Raju, who was hustling between the tables, told us, first, that this was his summer job. Now, the idea of a summer job having arrived in a village in Tamil Nadu got my attention. The second thing Raju said was that he was earning 450 rupees a month. That's about $15 a month. And he said that this was just enough for him to bicycle to the neighboring village in the evening, when he finished his work, to take computer classes.

So that 450 rupees paid for his computer education, which was done by a private company, called Aptech. And Raju said that his ambition in life was to run a computer company one day. And we asked Raju, where did you get this idea? He said, I saw it on TV. This man, his name is Billgay. He thought it was one word, "Billgay," he called him. He said, this man, that's my hero. He said, I'm going to be one day Billgay.

And then I knew at that point that India was changing and that what was changed more than anything else in the last 10 years was not just the reforms that had taken place but the young people's minds. And I came across dozens of stories, many of which I tell in the book, of young people who are like Raju. And the biggest change in India is I think amongst the young especially, but amongst a lot of people, where their minds, their dispositions, are different.

> *"Globalization creates growth by destruction of the environment and of local livelihoods. It therefore creates poverty."*

Global Capitalism Will Impoverish India

Vandana Shiva

Scientist and feminist activist Vandana Shiva is the founder and director of the India-based Research Foundation for Science, Technology, and Ecology. Her writings include the book *Biopiracy: The Plunder of Nature and Knowledge*. In the following viewpoint, she attacks the economic policies India adopted in the 1990s that promote free trade and capitalist reform. Such policies in her view have surrendered the control of India's economic and social welfare to foreign corporations, destroyed the livelihoods of millions of India's people, and degraded the environment. To preserve their future, the Indian people must act together to fight globalization, she concludes.

As you read, consider the following questions:
1. Why is "free trade" not really free, according to Shiva?
2. How has government deregulation of business affected the lives of Indians, in the author's opinion?
3. What local movements in India against foreign corporations does Shiva describe?

Vandana Shiva, "How Free Is Free India?" *Resurgence*, July/August 1997, pp. 14–17. Copyright © 1997 by Vandana Shiva. Reproduced by permission.

The war against diversity did not end with colonialism. With the definition of entire nations of people as undeveloped, incomplete and defective, Europeans were reincarnated in the "development" ideology, which predicated salvation on generous assistance and advice from the World Bank, the International Monetary Fund (IMF) and other financial institutions and multinational corporations.

Development is a beautiful word, which suggests evolution from within. It was, until the middle of the twentieth century, synonymous with self-organization. But the ideology of development has implied the globalization of the priorities, patterns and prejudices of the West. It has come to mean precisely the opposite of what the word originally meant. Instead of being self-generated, development is imposed. Instead of coming from within, it is externally guided. Instead of contributing to the maintenance of diversity it has meant the creation of homogeneity and uniformity. . . .

"Free trade" is the ruling metaphor for globalization in our times. But far from protecting the freedom of citizens and countries, free-trade negotiations and treaties have become the primary locations for the use of coercion and force. The cold war era has ended and the era of trade wars has begun.

Free trade is not free, because it operates in the economic interests of the powerful transnational corporations, which control 70% of world trade and for whom international trade is an imperative. Transnational corporate freedom is based on the destruction of citizen freedom everywhere. Globalization implies the dismantling of the powers of democratic institutions of individual countries—local councils, regional governments and parliaments.

Globalization and Accountability

While the Nehruvian era of state-directed development is being attacked by the globalizers and trade liberalizers, globalization is magnifying the problems of centralization: unaccountability, corruption, uniformity, inequality, environmental destruction and cultural erosion. Ever since the new economic policies were put in place in 1991 in response to the World Bank and IMF directives, decision-making has moved out of communities and regions to Delhi and then out of Delhi to Washington and Geneva and to corporate headquarters of transnational corporations (TNCs).

Unaccountability of government and corporations to people has increased. Corruption has exploded. Uniformity has expanded both ecologically and culturally. As agriculture gets corporatized, the landscape of small, biologically diverse farms is giving way to miles of monocultures of sunflowers, vegetables and shrimps for export. The McDonaldization of India has begun. Environmental destruction is taking place faster and over larger areas with globalization.

While globalization is strengthening the negative aspects of the development era, it is dismantling the positive aspects of a state focussing on the basic needs of people, a state committed to equality and justice, a state protecting resources and livelihoods through policy and regulatory mechanisms.

Basic needs have been replaced by import of luxury goods like cars and cosmetics and export of luxury products like flowers and shrimps. Land ceilings have been removed in urban and rural areas, transferring land and real estate to speculators or big corporations.

The livelihoods of small producers are being destroyed by trade liberalization. Two million weavers in Andhra Pradesh lost their livelihoods when free export of cotton was allowed, taking cotton beyond the access of weavers. 200,000 producers of Bikaneri Bhujia (a regional snack speciality) are threatened with the entry of Pepsico in the manufacture and marketing of Bikaneri Bhujia. New power plants have been established by bypassing the requirements of Environmental Impact Assessment. Deregulation does not imply an end to the state—it is a change in the function of the state. The state is now exclusively an instrument of global capital. . . .

Less Government?

The appeal of globalization is usually based on the idea that it implies less red tape, less centralization and less bureaucratic control. It is celebrated because it implies the erosion of the power of the state.

Globalization does mean "less government" for regulation of business and commerce. But less government for commerce and corporations can go hand-in-hand with more government in the lives of ordinary people. As globalization allows increasing transfer of resources from the public domain—either under the control of communities or that of the state—discontent increases, leading to law-and-order problems. In such a situation, even a minimalist state restricted only to policing will become enormously large and all-pervasive, devouring much of the wealth of society and intruding into every aspect of citizens' lives.

For example, under the new infrastructure policies, foreign companies can have 100% equity participation, but the government will acquire the land, displace people and deal with "law-and-order" problems created by displacements.

Most of the ideological projection of globalization has focussed on the new relationship of . . . the state and the corporation, the government and the market. The state has been stepping back more and more from the regulation of commerce and capital. Reflecting this ideology of deregulation, the Indian Finance Minister stated that "Power should move to the boardroom," i.e., from the state to the corporations. However, the shift from the rule of the nation-state to that of the corporations does not imply more power to the people. If anything, it implies less power in the hands of people, because transnational corporations are more powerful than governments and also because they are unaccountable to democratic control.

The erosion of the power of the nation-state leads to a concentration of power in the hands of corporations. It does not devolve power to the people. It does not move power downwards into the hands of communities. In fact, it takes power away from the local level and transforms institutions of the state from being protectors of the rights of people to being protectors of the profits of corporations. This creates an inverted state, a state more committed to the protection of foreign investment and less to the protection of the citizens of the country. The inversion of the state is well exemplified in a recently announced proposal that foreign security experts would train Indian police to protect the "life and property of foreign investors".

The expansion of corporate control is often made to appear as the expansion of the democratic space for citizens on the basis of "consumer choice". However, choice within a predetermined setup of options of corporate rule is not freedom, because it involves the surrender of the right to determine the context of living and the values that govern society. The apparent widening of individual consumer choice for the élite is based on the shrinking of the rights of communities to control their local resources and a shrinking of social choice through democratic process.

Freedom for Corporations, Not People

Globalization is creating more freedom for corporations. But this is not translating into more freedom for citizens.

Deregulation of commerce is not the same as reduced interferences by the state in the lives of citizens. "Self-governance" of corporations has very different social and political implications than self-governance of people. The end of the "licence raj" might imply more freedom for corporations to invest freely. But it also heralds the beginning of a "patent raj" in which governments are forced to play a new role of interfering in the lives of citizens—small producers, the farmers and craftspeople—to protect what big corporations have claimed as their "intellectual property"—seeds and medicinal plants.

It is often argued that globalization will create growth and growth will remove poverty. What is overlooked in this myth is that globalization creates growth by destruction of the environment and of local livelihoods. It therefore creates poverty instead of removing it. The new globalization policies have accelerated and expanded environmental destruction and displaced millions of people from their homes and their sustenance base.

The major democratic issue emerging in India is the right to survival of the large number of poor people who derive their livelihood from natural resources—land, water and biodiversity. In each sector, a major conflict is emerging between corporate control and community control over natural resources.

People's movements are demanding that power should not be concentrated in institutions of the centralized nation-states but should be distributed throughout society and should be dispersed through a multiplicity of institutions, with more power at the local level, controlled by local communities and their institutions. However, while the TNC-driven globalization agenda requires that power move from the centralized control of nation-states to the even more centralized control of global corporations and global institutions like the World Trade Organisation (WTO), the World Bank and the IMF, the people's democratically-driven agenda is for greater localization, both political and economic. Political localization implies more decisions being transferred to the local space. Economic localization implies that whatever can be produced locally with local resources should be part of the local economy so that both livelihoods and the environment are protected.

Against Unrestrained Globalization

While no one is arguing for India to remain aloof from the process of technological upgradation and modernization, it is unlikely that political and economic appeasement in the guise of globalization will do the trick for India. Unless India adopts a stance of hard bargaining and selectivity in the manner it globalizes, globalization will take place on the terms of the world's most powerful nations and is unlikely to bring widespread benefits for the Indian people. It is therefore high time that the mantra of unrestrained globalization be questioned and challenged. The tall claims made by its advocates need to be carefully scrutinized without the prevailing neo-liberal bias. The many failures, economic distortions and pitfalls of globalization need to be clearly exposed. Above all, India's economic policies need to be restructured to give an impetus to the local development of key technologies that play a crucial role in the modern economy and satisfy the most pressing needs of the vast majority of the Indian people.

South Asian Voice, August 2000.

While the international financial and trade organizations coerce and push the government into a blind and indiscriminate experiment with globalization, the Indian people are responding with a new politics of "localization". They are engaging in an enlightened response to put globalization in its ecological and social context. In region after region, where foreign investment is diverting local resources from survival needs of local people to the limitless appetite of global markets, people are putting investment to the test of ecological and social accountability. They are also redefining the principles of governance on the basis of decentralized democracy. The rule of the World Bank and the WTO has implied rule by super-state institutions serving the one-sided interest of commerce and beyond the democratic control of people. As the state withdraws from environmental and social regulation in the "free-trade" era, local communities are getting organized to regulate commercial activity by asserting their environmental rights to natural resources—land, water and biodiversity—and their democratic rights to decide how these resources are used.

They are redefining democracy in terms of people's decisions in their everyday lives. They are redefining the nation in terms of people, not in terms of the centralized state.

This trend towards localization has, in fact, been born along with the trend towards globalization. If globalization is the corporate-driven agenda for corporate control, localization is the countervailing citizens' agenda for protecting the environment and people's livelihoods. In the absence of regulation by national governments, citizens are creating a new politics, for introducing ecological limits. The movement for localization has an inbuilt environmental component of the sustainable use of local resources and an economic component to resist the destruction of local economies by the global economy and international trade.

Movements for Localization

Movements for localization are giving rise to a new people's protectionism. This is different from the old protectionism in the sense that power and authority to make environmental and economic decisions move from centralized states to structures of self-governance at the local level. Citizens and community organizations decide which roles and functions the state should have. In corporate protectionism all institutions of society—the courts, police, government departments—are distorted to protect the interests of transnational corporations, sacrificing the interests of citizens, small producers and small traders.

The largest corporations of the world have found new investment opportunities in India since 1991 . . . But now, in each sector, the biggest multinational corporation has been forced to recognize that it is the clearance from citizens, not just from the government, that is necessary for democratic functioning. . . .

The entry of TNCs, which threaten people's livelihoods, resources and health, is questioned by local communities and grassroots struggles. Local communities are raising a common voice: "We will decide the pattern of investment and development. We will determine the ownership and use of our natural resources." As this message resonates in village after village, from one investment site to another, a new environmental philosophy based on democratic decentralization of control over natural resources is emerging. The pressure of the people is forcing the government to remember its role as protector of the public interest and the country's natural and cultural heritage, not merely the interests of foreign investors. The tendency towards localization and deepening of democracy is aimed at taming the excesses of globalization, including the political excesses of deregulation.

The pattern that seems to be emerging is for environmental governance beyond the centralizing state and super-state systems, which work unidirectionally for the corporate interests. Localization is emerging as an antidote to globalization and to unrestrained commercial greed.

The re-emergence of democratic pluralism is putting justice and sustainability at the core of a new movement for freedom. Democratic pluralism is an alternative to both centralized and unaccountable state structures and centralized and unaccountable corporate structures. Globalization driven by transnational corporations creates a closed society: it is not an "opening up". It closes off the options of two-thirds of India—including the poor, the women, the tribals, the fishing communities, the peasants. It closes off India to her lasting strengths—diversity, pluralism, sustainability, simplicity and spirituality.

| "India's Hindu Nationalists have always resembled 1930s European fascists."

The Rise of Hindu Nationalism Threatens India's Future

Arun R. Swamy

In February and March 2002, violence between Hindus and Muslims in India's Gujarat state took hundreds of lives. In the following viewpoint, Arun R. Swamy argues that the tragic events in Gujarat (and the government's feeble response to them) is the fault of Hindu nationalist extremists who blame Muslims for India's problems and who have attained significant influence in Indian politics. Swamy, a research fellow at the East-West Center in Honolulu, Hawaii, argues that Hindu nationalism threatens to undermine or possibly even overturn India's democracy much as fascism took power in Germany in the 1930s.

As you read, consider the following questions:
1. What are the leading Hindu nationalist organizations, according to Swamy?
2. What similarities does the author see between contemporary India and Germany in the 1930s?
3. What must happen to prevent the rise of fascism in India, according to Swamy?

Arun R. Swamy, "Is India Going the Way of 1930's Germany?" *Foreign Policy in Focus*, March 26, 2002, pp. 1–3. Copyright © 2002 by Interhemispheric Resource Center (IRC). Reproduced by permission.

The recent rounds of violence [in February and March 2002] between religious groups in India do more than reveal the fragility of India's secular state. They highlight the inability of Indian democracy to combat what is essentially a fascist onslaught.

At first glance what happened in India appears to be another—if extreme—case of religious passion gone awry. A train carrying Hindu activists to the disputed religious site of Ayodhya was firebombed by a mob, killing 58 of the activists. Several days of revenge attacks by Hindus against Muslims followed in the state of Gujarat, killing over 700.

A Resemblance to Fascism

However, India's Hindu Nationalists have always resembled 1930s European fascists more than they do contemporary "fundamentalists." Members of the core organization of Hindu nationalism, the Rashtriya Swayamsevak Sangh (RSS), founded in the 1920s, are given paramilitary instruction, not religious, and wear khaki uniforms reminiscent of Mussolini's brownshirts. While the Vishwa Hindu Parishad (VHP), founded in the 1960s, is mainly concerned with religion, it still does not prescribe how Hindus should worship or behave—an impossible task given the diversity of Hindu religious practice.

Instead, like all Hindu nationalists, it is bent on characterizing *Muslims* as alien and hostile while seeking to unify Hindus around a romantic nationalism, in which military prowess plays a central role. Hindu nationalists' emphasis on international prestige has won them the support of the westernized middle class, typically the target of Islamic fundamentalism. Their focus on demonizing Muslims rather than promoting Hinduism is illustrated even by the dispute over Ayodhya, where extremist Hindu groups destroyed a 16th century Muslim mosque in 1992, sparking nationwide sectarian riots in which more than 2,000 people died.

Hindu nationalists claim that a temple on the same site honoring the birthplace of the Hindu deity, Rama, was torn down to make way for the mosque. For Hindu extremist groups the claim that a temple was torn down to build a mosque—for which there is no concrete evidence—was at least as important as the claim that Rama was born at the site. The destruction of the mosque was commonly spoken of in terms of retaking territory that had been lost to invaders. Hindu nationalists have identified other mosques they wish to destroy, claiming that these too were built on temple sites. For none do they claim the sanctity associated with the birthplace of Rama. Indeed, the purpose of claiming a particular site as Rama's birthplace—for which there is no basis in theology or tradition—was to justify tearing down the existing mosque.

It is this fascist ideology, and the fact that a party espousing it is at the head of the national government, that makes the recent anti-Muslim pogroms in Gujarat so much more disturbing than earlier rounds of riots. As horrific as the recent violence was, more died in 1992. But the political establishment's response this time has been ambivalent and feeble. The paralysis in the political system is emboldening the Hindu extremist organizations responsible for the Gujarat "riots" to press their agenda more forcefully. There are times when India seems to resemble Germany in the 1920s and early 1930s.

Government Failures

The analogy to the rise of Hitler is not one that should be made lightly, but there are many parallels. The Gujarat attacks were not spontaneous expressions of mob rage but were highly organized and brutally efficient, probably identifying Muslim homes and businesses through the use of public records. The state government was almost certainly complicit in the wave of violence that affected the entire state and saw no effort by the police to control it. The central government was slow to dispatch the army, and has attempted to put the focus on the train attack, for which they blame Pakistani intelligence.

The state government initially sought to limit judicial inquiry to investigating the train attack, to use its emergency powers only against those accused of the train attack, and to offer higher levels of compensation to the (Hindu) victims of the train attack on the grounds that they were victims of terrorism. Even many liberal intellectuals and politicians, whose protests forced the state government to retract some of these measures, have tacitly accepted the idea that several days of targeted anti-Muslim violence can be equated with the attack on the train, and even resulted from it.

Worse, there has been no effort by those in power to hold those responsible for the Gujarat attacks accountable. The national government, run by the same party as the state government, the Bharatiya Janata Party (BJP), has chosen not to use its constitutional authority to take over the state's administration despite having attempted last year to do so on law and order grounds in another, opposition-ruled state. Although the government has banned militant Islamic groups, it has ignored calls by parties both in the opposition

---

A Hindu Theocracy

"The 21st century will belong to Hindus" was the claim made by extreme right-wing group leader Kuppahalli Sitharamaiya Sudarshan, chief of the Rashtriya Swayamsevak Sangh (RSS), while addressing about 75,000 RSS activists attending the last day of a three-day event held in Agra, India, to mark the group's 75th anniversary. . . .

Sudarshan, overwhelmed by the show of force of his group's activists in such a large number, came out with the baneful sentiment of religious hate, prejudice and intolerance against Christians and Muslims and called upon them to acknowledge their common Hindu ancestry as the 21st century would be shaped and dominated by Hindus. He further added, "Christianity is less of a religion and is more about politics. It is detrimental to the interests of our country."

The agenda of the RSS is well-known. They want a Hindu theocracy in India. They have always believed that the real India is a Hindu India. The threats posed to Indian society, particularly members of Christian, Muslim and Sikh minorities, cannot be taken lightly as the Bhartiya Janata Party (BJP), head of the ruling political alliance in India, has close links with the RSS. The presence of the BJP's home minister, Lal Krishna Advani, on the third day of the RSS meetings further caused a matter of concern over the Hindu right-wing agenda to theocratise India and subjugate non-Hindus. Advani's participation clearly sends messages of more communal conflict in India in the days to come.

Naeem Shakir, *Human Rights Solidarity*, April 2001.

and in its own coalition to do this to Hindu extremist organizations. The involvement of these organizations in the Gujarat violence is widely attested to, and they were banned after they tore down the Ayodhya mosque in 1992.

Worse still, even *after* the Gujarat riots the government negotiated with the VHP over its plans to begin construction of a temple on the disputed site. The compromise involved an official in the Prime Minister's Office accepting possession of two pillars intended for inclusion in the temple structure. Even though this seriously compromised the Indian state's claims to religious neutrality, the government has congratulated itself for defusing a potentially explosive situation.

To be sure, the government is in a tight spot. BJP members of parliament have expressed outrage at the government's refusal to let temple construction proceed until the Supreme Court rules on the subject. However, statements and actions by Hindu extremist organizations since suggest that they have been emboldened by the concessions the government has made. Over the weekend of March 15 members of several right-wing Hindu organizations stormed and sacked the legislative assembly of the state of Orissa for unknown reasons, while the RSS warned Indian Muslims that their safety depended on the goodwill of the Hindu majority. The next week the VHP indicated that it had plans to carry the ashes of the train attack victims in processions throughout the country—an act calculated to incite mob fury. It later disavowed its plans when many of the BJP's coalition allies threatened to pull out of the coalition if the plans were carried through.

Opposition Parties

The opposition parties and some of the BJP's coalition allies have succeeded in checking the VHP to some degree. They have called for Hindu extremist organizations to be banned, and condemned the compromise with the VHP over the performance of the temple ceremony, as well as the attack on the Orissa assembly and the RSS' statement on Muslims. In addition to blocking the alleged plans to carry the ashes of Hindus killed in the train attack in a procession many have threatened to withdraw their support if the Ayodhya temple is built. The BJP leadership has promised to abide by the Supreme Court's ruling on the temple site. However, the VHP can undertake many provocative acts short of actually constructing the temple and has announced plans for more religious ceremonies centering on the temple issue around the country. There is a limit to how many battles the allies can fight and win from within the government.

The BJP's allies have been reluctant to withdraw from the government and indeed, voted with the government in passing a Prevention of Terrorism Bill that will significantly weaken protections for civil liberties including allowing confessions extorted from prisoners by police to be admitted as evidence. The Act, the provisions of which are currently in operation as an executive order, was defeated in the upper house of parliament where the opposition parties are in a majority, but it then passed in an unusual joint session of parliament. During the acrimonious debate two former prime ministers charged that the existing ordinance was used selectively against Muslims in Gujarat, while the current Leader of the Opposition, Sonia Gandhi, argued that the law would be used by the national government to intimidate its opponents and divide the country.

Short-term political calculations keep the government in power. Most of the BJP's allies are regional parties. The opposition Congress Party, which has won a string of recent elections is their local rival. Similar divisions between the Congress and other opposition parties have also hindered efforts to form an alternate coalition. Indeed, some opposition parties are gravitating toward the government out of tactical considerations even as some of its allies pull away from it. Meanwhile the two communist parties, outwardly the most opposed to the BJP, have announced that they would refuse to support a Congress government because of differences with that party's economic policy.

Reducing Space for Dissent

This combination of organized thugs affiliated with the ruling party who terrorize a minority community and intimidate a silent majority, with a divided opposition in which the center is getting squeezed from both sides, is only the most obvious parallel to Germany in the early 1930s. Over the past few years, the BJP has tried to reshape the secondary school curriculum by stealth in ways that fit with Hindu nationalist ideology and has presided over the slow militarization of the polity. By casting the Pakistan-supported insurgency in Kashmir as a crisis of national security, military expenditures have been increased while social welfare expenses have been cut. The command structure of the armed forces, which were kept divided for decades to ensure civilian control, has been unified in recent years. With the passage of the Prevention of Terrorism Bill, the government will have most of the tools it requires to gradually reduce the space for dissent.

There are many factors that could prevent this from happening. The Supreme Court has blocked both the VHP's plans for Ayodhya and the release of new textbooks following the social studies curricula. The National Human Rights Commission, which in India has some judicial powers, has rejected the Gujarat government's initial report on the riots as "perfunctory" and demanded a more thorough accounting. With the opposition parties controlling the presidency, upper house of parliament, most state governments, and therefore the electoral college for electing the next president this summer, it would be difficult for the BJP to significantly alter the constitutional balance or to declare a state of national emergency. Moreover, the government has a stake in preserving India's credentials as a secular state, in order to maintain U.S. pressure on neighboring Pakistan to crack down on militant Islamic groups and in order to develop economic ties with Islamic countries like Iran. Continued provocations by Hindu extremist organizations could yet force a rift between the BJP and its allies or even within the BJP, which is divided over the temple issue.

A Broader Trend

However, the difficulty India's mainstream parties have had in maintaining a united opposition to the BJP's agenda, and the change in the international attitude toward civil liberties following [the September 11, 2001, terrorist attacks], make it difficult to feel confident that Hindu fascism will be defeated.

For this to happen, both centrist parties in the ruling coalition, and India's friends abroad will need to recognize that what happened in Gujarat was not just another instance of religious communities in conflict. Rather, as Indian opposition leaders have charged, it was part of a broader tendency toward eliminating civil liberties and scapegoating cultural minorities in an aggressive effort to impose a unified sense of nationhood on one of the world's most culturally diverse societies.

"The whole idea of the 'Hindu right' is a ploy to discredit the Hindu movement."

The Threat of Hindu Nationalism Is Exaggerated

Part I: David Frawley; Part II: Sarita Sarvate

The following two-part viewpoint features articles that examine and defend Hindu activism in India. In Part I, David Frawley argues that labeling the Hindu movement as right-winged or even fascist is misleading and unfairly dismissive. Hindus in India seek to protect their traditional culture and spirituality against western religious and commercial interests. Frawley is the founder and director of the American Institute of Vedic Studies; his books include *How I Became a Hindu: My Discovery of Vedic Dharma* and *Hinduism and the Clash of Civilizations*. In Part II, Sarita Sarvate argues that Hindu nationalism is becoming increasingly popular and accepted in India, and that Indian Hindus have legitimate concerns and grievances that should be acknowledged by American foreign-policy makers and others. Sarvate is a writer for *India Currents* and other publications.

As you read, consider the following questions:
1. How is the Hindu cause similar to that of other native and tribal peoples, according to Frawley?
2. How does Frawley characterize Hindu economics?
3. What evidence of a resurgence in Indian nationalism does Sarvate cite?

I

In media accounts today, any group that identifies itself as Hindu or tries to promote any Hindu cause is immediately and uncritically defined as 'right-winged'. In the leftist accounts that commonly come from the Indian press, Hindu organizations are also routinely called militants and fascists. However, if we look at their actual views, Hindu groups have a very different ideology and practices than the political right in other countries. In fact many Hindu causes are more at home in the left in the West than in the right.

The whole idea of the 'Hindu right' is a ploy to discredit the Hindu movement as backward and prevent people from really examining it. The truth is that the Hindu movement is a revival of a native spiritual tradition that has nothing to do with the political right-wing of any western country. Its ideas are spiritually evolutionary, not politically regressive, though such revivals do have a few extremists. Let us examine the different aspects of the Hindu movement and where they would fall in the political spectrum of left and right as usually defined in the West.

Hinduism and Native Traditions

The Hindu cause is similar to the causes of native and tribal peoples all over the world, like Native American and African groups. Even Hindu concerns about cultural encroachment by western religious and commercial interests mirrors those of other traditional peoples who want to preserve their cultures. Yet while the left has taken up the concerns of native peoples worldwide, the same concerns of Hindus are styled right-wing or communal, particularly in India!

When native Americans ask for a return of their sacred sites, the left in America supports them. When Hindus ask for a similar return of their sacred sites, the left in India opposes them and brands them as intolerant for their actions! When native peoples in America or Africa protest against the missionaries for interfering with their culture, the left supports them. Yet when Hindus express the same sentiments, the left attacks them. Even the Hindu demand for rewriting the history of India to better express the value of their indigenous traditions is the same as what native Africans and

Americans are asking for. Yet the left opposes this Hindu effort, while supporting African and American efforts of a similar nature.

In countries like America, native traditions are minorities and thereby afforded a special sympathy. Leftists in general tend to support minority causes and often lump together black African and native American causes as examples of the damage caused by racism and colonialism. In India, a native tradition has survived the colonial period but as the tradition of the majority of the people. Unfortunately, the intellectual elite of India, though following largely a leftist orientation, has no sympathy for the country's own native tradition. They identify it as right-wing in order to express their hostility towards it. They try to portray it as a majority oppression of minorities, when it is the movement of a suppressed majority to regain its dignity.

Not surprisingly, the same leftists in India, who have long been allied to communist China, similarly styled the Dalai Lama and the Tibetan cause as right-wing and regressive, though the Dalai Lama is honored by the American left. This should tell the reader about the meaning of right and left as political terms in India.

When one looks at the Hindu movement as the assertion of a native tradition with a profound spiritual heritage, the whole perspective on it changes.

Hindu Economics

The Hindu movement in India in its most typical form follows a Swadeshi (own-country) movement like the Swadeshi Jagaran Manch. It emphasizes protecting the villages and local economies, building economic independence and self-reliance for the country. It resists corporate interference and challenges multinational interests, whether the bringing of fast food chains to India, western pharmaceuticals or terminator seeds.

Such an economic policy was supported by Mahatma Gandhi with his emphasis on the villages, reflected in his characteristic usage of the spinning wheel. Its counterparts in the West are the groups that protest the World Trade Organization (WTO), the World Bank and the International

Monetary Fund (IMF). However, these protest groups are generally classified as 'left-wing' by the international press.

The international press considers the economic right-wing to be the powers of the multinational corporations, particularly, the oil industry, which certainly are not the allies of Hindu economics.

Clearly Hindu economics is more connected with the New Left in the West and has little in common with the right. The Republican right in America, with its corporate interests, would hardly take up the cause of Hindu economics either.

Meanwhile the BJP, the so-called Hindu nationalist party in India, has been responsible for much of the economic liberalization of the country, sometimes even to the dismay of some votaries of Hindu economics. It has been the main opponent of the socialist policies of the previous Congress and left governments that had communist leanings. While such a movement is to the right in the political spectrum, the policies of the BJP are a movement towards western capitalism from the left, they are not a movement from it to the right.

II

Long marginalized, Hindu nationalism is becoming mainstream in India.

The burning of an Indian train headed for Ayodhya, the birthplace of the God Ram, has once more flared Hindu sentiments in the subcontinent.

During a recent visit, I found liberals and intellectuals, jet setters and slum dwellers, men and women, Brahmins and untouchables expressing this Hindu pride.

I think it is history's revenge for a land that was subjugated by foreigners for over 1,000 years.

It was Mahmud of Ghazni from Afghanistan who first came roaring through the Khyber Pass around 1000 AD to destroy the magnificent Hindu temple at Somnath. These early Muslim rulers of India were soon followed by other dynasties, all with connections to Afghanistan.

Because of its polytheistic, pacifist and non-proselytizing nature, Hinduism became vulnerable to the coming of Islam. Muslims ruled India until the 1600s, when the British took over.

Hindutva

Hindutva, or the Hindu fundamentalist movement, originally began in the back alleys of my hometown of Nagpur in 1926, in the wake of India's struggle for freedom from British rule. Through the recitation of stories of native heroes like Shivaji, who had successfully fought guerrilla warfare against the Mughal despot Aurangzeb, the movement strove to incite nationalistic pride in a people who had lost their identity.

Responses to Criticism

If there are two oft-repeated criticisms which irritate India's Hindu nationalist RSS, one is that it admired Hitler and the other is that one of its former members assassinated independence leader Mahatma Gandhi.

"Mischievous propaganda," says the national spokesman of the Rashtriya Swayamsevak Sangh (RSS), or National Volunteer Corps, which has been campaigning for Hindu nationalism since it was founded to fight British colonial rule in 1925.

The ideological parent of the ruling Bharatiya Janata Party (BJP), the RSS also denies its Hindu nationalism is anti-Muslim.

"All Hindus are tolerant," said Madhav Govind Vaid in an interview this week. "But there are some things of which you should be intolerant. Should we tolerate intolerance also? And should we allow people to abuse and exploit our tolerance?"

Myra MacDonald, *Yahoo News*, April 26, 2002.

The partition of the country at independence from Britain created deeper wounds in the Hindu psyche. Later, America's support for military dictatorships in Pakistan and the simultaneous marginalizing of India, the world's largest democracy, kept the Hindutva movement alive.

Now, the war on terrorism has opened these 1,000-year-old wounds once again. Indians, who were hoping for strong American rhetoric against Taliban-incited terrorism in Kashmir in the wake of [the September 11, 2001, terrorist attacks on America], were sorely disappointed. Many Hindus today believe that U.S. concern for victims of terrorism is limited only to its citizens, and does not extend to innocent Indians.

Most Indians I spoke to clearly believe that Kashmir—a majority-Moslim region between India and Pakistan—belongs to India.

Nationalistic Pride

This nationalistic pride was revealed to me when a Bengali friend—who hails from a cosmopolitan and Westernized family and to whom I had always looked up to during my formative years for guidance on American literature, art, music and pop culture—told me about a recent pilgrimage she had undertaken to the holy city of Varanasi. As she was bathing in the waters of the Ganges, she said, what struck her was not the spectacle of hundreds of little Hindu temples dotting the riverbank, but the shadow of the enormous mosque built by Aurangzeb still towering over the holy site.

In that instance, I realized that what Hindus need today from the international community is an acknowledgment of the legitimacy of Hindu nationalism in a historical context. Such understanding is essential for any agreement on Kashmir that will pass muster with Indians.

Indeed, 50 years after independence from Britain, many Indians invoke memories of past invasions so that future generations will not be too pacifistic.

"You can turn the other cheek for only so long. Sometimes you have to show the world that you are proud," a female friend commented during my visit.

Women and Hinduism

Educated women seem to be on the forefront of the Hindu nationalistic movement today. Many now join peasants in their annual trek to the Kumbh Mela and other spiritual gatherings.

Unless future American foreign policy takes Hindu nationalism into account, violence in the subcontinent may well escalate, and might lead to a military, even a nuclear, conflict.

Standing in the visa line at the Indian Consulate in San Francisco recently, I noticed the large picture of the Taj Mahal covering an entire wall. "Isn't it ironic," I said to a friend, "that the one icon most people identify with India happens to be a Muslim tomb?"

"I wish they would use a picture of the Minakshi Temple instead," she replied. The temple is Hindu.

And then we both fell silent, surprised by our own non-secular sentiments.

But such sentiments are not uncommon among Indian immigrants, many of whom believe that America needs to take a more favorable stance with regard to India, the world's largest democracy, vis-à-vis Pakistan, a military dictatorship harboring Taliban terrorists.

| "*Musharraf looks set to become the second dictator to break political and militant Islam for the sake of democracy.*"

Military Dictatorship May Be Necessary to Save Pakistan from Islamic Fundamentalism

David Pryce-Jones

In 1999, General Pervez Musharraf overthrew Pakistan's civilian government in a coup. While he has been criticized by some both within and outside of Pakistan for failing to restore democracy in that country, David Pryce-Jones argues in the following viewpoint that Musharraf should instead be praised for taking actions against Islamic militants in Pakistan. He compares Musharraf to Mustapha Kemal (Ataturk), who as military dictator of Turkey following World War I successfully established the foundations for a secular society and democratic government in that country. Pryce-Jones contends that a similar period of military rule may be necessary in Pakistan to prevent the country from succumbing to Islamic extremism or descending into anarchy. A senior editor for the conservative magazine *National Review*, Pryce-Jones is a historian and author whose books include *A Closed Circle: An Interpretation of the Arabs*.

As you read, consider the following questions:

1. What does Pryce-Jones argue about the creation of Pakistan in 1947?
2. What decision did General Musharraf have to make following September 11, 2001, according to the author?

David Pryce-Jones, "Ataturk II?" *National Review*, vol. 54, February 25, 2002, pp. 32–34. Copyright © 2002 by National Review, Inc. Reproduced by permission.

General Pervez Musharraf is every inch a professional soldier. On October 12, 1999, he was army chief of staff in Pakistan and flying home from a visit to Sri Lanka. He had recently fired a senior officer for meeting the Pakistani prime minister Nawaz Sharif without permission. Musharraf was pleased with himself; but Sharif felt insulted. A power struggle was underway.

Calculating that Musharraf couldn't do much about it in mid-air, Sharif fired him. Wrong. Landing at Karachi airport, Musharraf arranged a coup, put Sharif on trial, and sent him into exile in Saudi Arabia. Musharraf installed himself in Sharif's place. That's the way politics are conducted pretty much throughout the Muslim world. Personalities in this context are real, while principles are nebulous.

The military is the one and only institution in Pakistan that can be said to function. It is unwise to tamper with it. Military coups occur at regular intervals, and the country has had long spells under martial law—without which it would have disintegrated into anarchy. An assortment of different peoples and languages are engaged in permanent jostling, without benefit of democracy or the rule of law. Government writ does not hold in the northwest frontier where [the terrorist network] al-Qaeda and maybe [terrorist] Osama bin Laden could be sheltering. In major cities like Lahore and Karachi, people die regularly in obscure shootings, whether committed by political extremists or criminals. Civil society does not exist. What has brought these people together is only the chance that they are all Muslims.

A British Blunder

In the words of a famous clerihew, that peculiar but pointed verse from, "George the Third / Ought never to have occurred. / One can only wonder / At so grotesque a blunder." Pakistan ought never to have occurred either, and one can only wonder at the way the British manufactured it without regard to what they themselves believed, and ignoring the experience of two centuries of empire.

Governing the Indian subcontinent, the British were careful to keep the balance between Hindus and Muslims. Although predisposed by temperament to favor the Muslims—who seemed to them livelier and more capable than the Hindus—they administered the law impartially, and laid the basis for the democracy that India itself is now perpetuating. Responsible Muslim leaders were on equal terms with their Hindu counterparts, and Muslim extremism appeared to be a thing of the past.

At the start of the 20th century, the British honored a promise to initiate a public debate about the coming of self-rule for the peoples of the empire. In a reaction that surprised them, this provoked an identity crisis everywhere. From India to Egypt to Ireland, the resulting wave of nationalism is still working itself out. Hindus had their National Congress, and Muslims should have been encouraged to join it in a power-sharing spirit. Instead, one of the viceroy's advisers, a man with the resonant name of William Shakespear, suggested that Muslims should form a counterpart, known as the Muslim League.

Out of such seeds were to grow the division of the subcontinent into two religious and national communities contending for supremacy in fear of each other; then three countries (with Bangladesh splitting away from Pakistan—probably one day there will be a fourth country, Kashmir); and so incessant warfare; and now finally a nuclear standoff. In 1947, the British agreed to partition and immediately scuttled home ashamed of themselves, to allow all on the ground to do their worst and finalize the horrors to come. Millions of people were left at one another's throat.

Why independent India succeeded while independent Pakistan failed is a question inviting many answers, having to do with religion and culture, expectation, circumstances, bad government, and various imponderables. In one of his penetrating phrases, V.S. Naipaul has written that to most Muslims the state that had been won out of the subcontinent came "as a kind of religious ecstasy, something beyond reason, beyond quibbles about borders and constitutions." Nothing to do with democracy, the Muslim League and other political parties have been so many religious or ethnic mass movements whereby ambitious individuals lever themselves into absolute power.

The ruling elite has mercilessly exploited the religious ecstasy that came with the birth of the state. Pakistan today is second only to Saudi Arabia as a source of Islamic militancy. Islam provides an identity above ethnicity, tribe, or clan. Some 7,000 madrassahs, or religious seminaries, fanaticize otherwise uneducated boys by teaching them to memorize the Koran in Arabic (which is not their language, and which they do not understand), and no other subjects at all. Thousands of mullahs preach incendiary sermons in order to mobilize the mob against unbelievers. In the supposed cause of Islam, successive rulers have sponsored and exploited a variety of militant groups, notably the Taliban in Afghanistan, and Jaish-e-Muhammad and Lashkar-e-Taiba to terrorize Kashmir. The military and its most powerful agency, the Inter-Services Intelligence force, the ISI, exploited Islamic extremism by means of a doctrine of "strategic depth" whose purpose was to spread Pakistani influence in Kashmir and throughout Central Asia.

Reckless adventure of this sort has generated corruption and a foreign policy based on terror, carrying the recurrent risk of war with India and other neighbors. Every method, including assassination, has been used to silence intellectual opponents and dissidents, and to cow the population at large. An undeclared civil war rages between Islamic militants and secular-minded moderates. Equally caught up in its vision of religious ecstasy and equally indifferent to the fate of the masses, the ruling elite in Saudi Arabia has oil wealth at its disposal, while in Pakistan debt servicing already accounts for over half the budget. The country is on the edge of bankruptcy. Two emotional foreign policies fused when Saudi Arabia financed Pakistan to build the "Islamic nuclear bomb" that destabilizes the region far and wide.

Musharraf's coup was bloodless, and widely welcomed in long-suffering and lawless Pakistan. To brake the descent of his country into the abyss, he would need all the powers at his disposal, however arbitrary and undemocratic these might be. The Clinton administration's reaction, however, was to "seek the earliest possible restoration of democracy in Pakistan." The State Department spokesman said that "Pakistan's constitution must be respected, not only in the letter but in its spirit." This was fantasy, as though the Pakistani constitution were like the American. In Pakistan, the constitution is what the ruler, the army, and the ISI decide it is. The British were equally comical and ignorant in their response. Robin Cook, the foreign secretary at the time, deplored the coup, and Peter Hain, a reliably wrong-headed junior minister, gave the empty boast that "Britain will act very firmly to ensure Pakistan receives no international support and is penalized as strongly as possible diplomatically."

Pakistan's President Speaks Against Islamic Extremism

Pakistan is our land. It is our soil. If we forsake it, we will face difficulties. This lesson we must learn.

Sectarian terrorism has been going on for years. Everyone of us is fed up with it. It is becoming unbearable. Our peace-loving people are keen to get rid of the Klashinkov and weapon culture. Every one is sick of it. It was because of this that we banned Lashkar-e-Jhangvi and Sipah-e-Muhammad. [two groups linked to terrorist acts in India]. Yet little improvement occurred. The day of reckoning has come. Do we want Pakistan to become a theocratic state? Do we believe that religious education alone is enough for governance or do we want Pakistan to emerge as a progressive and dynamic Islamic welfare state? The verdict of the masses is in favour of a progressive Islamic state. This decision, based on the teaching of the Holy Prophet (Peace Be Upon Him). . . will put Pakistan on the path of progress and prosperity.

President Pervez Musharraf's address to the nation, January 12, 2002.

For Islamic militants in Pakistan, the [September 11, 2001, terrorist attacks on America] signified that their hour of triumph had come. In a spasm of religious ecstasy, thousands rushed to join the Taliban and al-Qaeda, and many tens of thousands mobilized in the cities for demonstrations that were almost uprisings. Musharraf at once understood that he was between a rock and a hard place: He had to decide which side he was on in the undeclared civil war between Islamic extremists and secular moderates. This was nothing less than an existential choice over the future of Pakistan.

All other leaders in Muslim countries have confronted this same choice about the ultimate role of Islam and Islamic militants. They have made sure to assert full control by such means as setting up an official ministry responsible for the appointment of mullahs and preachers, and nationalizing religious property. Should skillful maneuvers of this kind fail, they have not hesitated to suppress and eliminate their Islamists with whatever violent means available, including massacres, judicial executions, and life sentences in prison. What they cannot tolerate is the threat posed to their dictatorship by Islamic extremists.

The Turkish Precedent

Mustapha Kemal, otherwise known as Ataturk, or "father of the Turks," set the first and most striking precedent. The Ottoman Empire had been the foremost Muslim power in the world until its defeat in the First War. The one and only successful Ottoman general in that war, Ataturk afterwards staged a bloodless coup to seize power for himself and to use it in order to constitute modern Turkey out of the wreckage. Islam, in his view, was a total obstacle to modernization and had to be reformed out of all recognition. Andrew Mango, his authoritative biographer, calls him a freethinker, and quotes him saying to a reporter, "I have no religion, and at times I wish all religions at the bottom of the sea. He is a weak ruler who needs religion to uphold his people . . . My people are going to learn the principles of democracy, the dictates of truth, and the teachings of science. Superstition must go. Let them worship as they will; every man can follow his own conscience."

The aim was to disestablish Islam. A new Ministry of Religious Affairs allowed Ataturk to administer Islam and the mullahs for his purposes. Using strong-arm methods where necessary, he closed the madrassahs and suppressed the extremist orders of dervishes. He is said personally to have punched recalcitrant mullahs and to have ordered the destruction of a mosque that spoiled his view. His fondness for alcohol and womanizing was no secret. Traditional Islamic dress, including the veil for women, was outlawed. After he had finished, Islam was no longer the official state religion, and the foundations of secularism were well and truly laid. Turkey has since changed its government through democratic election, as Ataturk intended. True, in recent times there have been military coups and interludes of martial law. True too, Islamic extremists have made a comeback, and even formed a government, and the secular parties have resorted to undemocratic stratagems to keep them out of politics. Even with these imperfections, Turkey today may claim to be the one and only Muslim country with any democratic credentials.

Musharraf is now in the Ataturk position, a dictator deploying absolute power for the apparently paradoxical ends of modernizing and democratizing. Like Ataturk, he has to work in chaotic conditions to create a nation-state capable of dealing with the difficulties it faces. He made his existential choice when he broke with the Taliban, joined the American coalition, and opened local air bases to American aircraft. He has also purged senior generals in the army and the ISI who were Islamists and promoters of the "strategic depth" doctrine that has wreaked such havoc. He has banned Jaish-e-Muhammad and Lashkar-e-Taiba and several other terror groups as well, closing 500 of their offices and ordering the tracking of their funds with the aim of freezing them. In the most fraught part of this U-turn, he has had arrested an estimated 2,000 militants who until now were secretly subsidized and encouraged by the ISI. He describes madrassahs correctly as places that "propagate hatred and violence," and in the future they will have to register with the authorities and teach modern courses. Rival politicians and influential opinion-makers who hitherto have criticized Musharraf for usurping democratic rule are now coming around to him because Pakistan has changed course and will not become an extremist Islamist state. Democracy, he told the nation in a televised broadcast, is the long-term objective.

Islam and democracy, as Ataturk discovered, prove to be incompatible ideals. Musharraf looks set to become the second dictator to break political and militant Islam for the sake of democracy. This requires personal courage, and the successful outcome of the American war on terror. Democratizing Pakistan, he would also be in a position to abate the grotesque blunder of partitioning British India on religious lines. It is a tall order, but he has a chance to go down in history as a great man.

"Far from being besieged by Islamic extremists, Pakistan's military government has carefully used [them] . . . to justify its hold on power."

Pakistan's Military Government Threatens Its Future

International Crisis Group

The International Crisis Group (ICG) is a private organization of field researchers and scholars that provides analyses on issues related to international crisis management. In the following viewpoint, members of ICG assess the actions of Pakistan's government, and its leader, Pervez Musharraf. They argue that conventional wisdom about Pakistan—that it is a fragile state that could fall under the control of Islamic extremists, that Musharraf has taken a courageous stand against these extremists, and that the international community should support him—does not bear close scrutiny. They contend that Islamic fundamentalism actually has little popular support among Pakistan's people and that Pakistan's military establishment uses the threat of militant Islam to justify its size and actions. Pakistan's future would be best assured by economic development, education, and establishing the rule of law—all of which are unlikely to happen as long as the military maintains its dominant position in Pakistan.

As you read, consider the following questions:

1. How did Pakistan's international standing change on September 11, 2001, according to the ICG?
2. According to the ICG, how does the military prevent Pakistan from addressing its most pressing problems?

F ew nations have been more dramatically thrust into the spotlight since [the September 11, 2001, terrorist attacks on America] than Pakistan. Prior to that date, Pakistan found itself increasingly isolated as a result of a number of factors including fairly transparent military and security support for both the Taliban [the fundamentalist Islamic rulers of Afghanistan] and militant cross border insurgents in Kashmir, a military takeover of government in October 1999 and deep and persistent economic difficulties.

In the immediate aftermath of the terrorist attacks in New York and Washington, the government of General Pervez Musharraf was directly pressured to cooperate with the Bush administration on a range of issues including condemning the 11 September attacks and assisting in the destruction of terrorist Osama bin Laden and the al-Qaeda network, ending support for the Taliban, granting blanket overflight and landing rights and access to Pakistani military bases, and offering intelligence assistance and logistical support. Pakistan moved quickly to assure the United States that it would offer full cooperation, and it was deemed an essential partner in the war on terrorism. . . .

The current high praise for the Musharraf government is driven both by appreciation for measures it has taken and by fears of possible alternatives. Western officials, analysts and reporters have warned direly of that government's fragile state and suggested that it could succumb to angry street protests or swelling Islamic extremism. Similarly, much has been made of the influence of extreme Islamic religious parties within Pakistan's political system and public life. Others have pointed to potential splits between the country's military and its Directorate for Inter-Services Intelligence (ISI) in trying to explain Pakistan's long running support for Islamic extremist groups. All these points are often combined, when viewed against the backdrop of efforts to cooperate with the West since 11 September, to suggest that the Musharraf government has made a fundamental strategic and philosophical shift in recent months.

Unfortunately, many of these claims do not stand up under closer scrutiny. They require glossing over the symbiotic relationship between Pakistan's military and security services and Islamic extremists in recent years as well as the desire of the country's generals to maintain their institution's central role in political life. Far from being besieged by Islamic extremists, Pakistan's military government has carefully used that phenomenon as an essential tool to justify its hold on power, improve its standing with the West, and resist restoring secular democracy and as a tactical means to advance its goals in both Afghanistan and Kashmir. . . .

A Government on the Brink?

Top officials are adamant that the government's decision to side with the U.S. is a moral stand against terrorism. But they also say President Pervez Musharraf must be rewarded for his gamble—or risk losing public support to the angry mullahs calling for a jihad against America.

USA Today
5 October 2001

One of the first pieces of conventional wisdom regarding Pakistan to take a direct hit [after September 11, 2001] was the notion that an angry "Pakistani street" was waiting to rise up against the military government if it cooperated with the West. As events unfolded, street protests were relatively few, not well attended and short lived. However, the military government was able to use the threat of such unrest to help leverage wider benefits for its cooperation, and President Musharraf was able to portray himself as a bold leader taking a stand against religious extremism.

However, the fizzle of street protests should come as no surprise. It has traditionally been Pakistan's military that has played a lead role in encouraging religious parties to take to the streets when it saw fit for such protests to be held. Far from being under direct siege by the more extreme religious parties, the military and these parties have enjoyed a long running and symbiotic relationship. It is also important to note that Pakistan's military, while relying heavily on such elements to achieve certain goals, remains a largely secular force with little interest in embracing a fundamentalist religious worldview—making its approach all the more cynical.

The military and intelligence services have used these parties to promote their agenda in several important ways. According to a former chief of ISI, General Hameed Gul,

"Religious forces have always aligned themselves with the military's views with regard to the defense budget [and] the Kashmir and Afghan policies". Pakistan's military leaders supported the Taliban to attain their goal of strategic depth in Afghanistan by squeezing out the interests of other regional rivals including Iran and India . . .

Support for the Taliban and religious parties within Pakistan also let the government take potential steam out of a move for a unified Pashtun territory stretching across the borders of Afghanistan and Pakistan. Religious extremists trained and funded in Afghanistan by Pakistan were also seen as an important tool by which to "bleed" India in Kashmir through cross border insurgency. The logic was simple: if Pakistan could make the cost of holding Kashmir high enough for India by helping to sponsor a long running guerrilla campaign, New Delhi would eventually offer a fundamentally favourable deal at the negotiating table.

A Former Prime Minister's View

[Pakistan's prime minister Pervez] Musharraf has a record of disingenuous manipulation of world public opinion at the expense of basic human and democratic rights. Although he now denounces the contours of a theocratic state in Pakistan, he and his establishment supporters have yet to dismantle the governmental structure on which it rests. Though he now claims containment of terrorists and militants, for years he turned a blind eye to the Islamic groups Lashkar-e-Tayyaba and Jaish-e-Mohammad, which many believe were involved in the Dec. 13 [2001] attack on the Indian Parliament.

Musharraf now denounces Pakistan's "state within a state"—the Inter-Services Intelligence, or ISI—while he and his military predecessors tasked the ISI to destabilize democratic government in Pakistan and manipulate the electoral process. He denounces the Islamicization of Pakistan, while for years the exploitation of Islam has been the military's way of stifling the Pakistani people. . . .

Only an internationally monitored, free and fair, party-based election open to all political parties—including the Pakistan People's Party, which I chair—can create the legitimacy that would derail the fundamentalists' dream of a theocratic state.

Benazir Bhutto, *Christian Science Monitor*, February 5, 2002.

The military government has also used its support for extremist groups to advance its domestic and international agendas. The military and intelligence services have employed extremist elements as a convenient tool with which to bludgeon mainstream political parties when they are seen as becoming too powerful or moving in directions contrary to the perceived interests of the military establishment. By pointing to the twin threats of religious extremism and political party corruption, the military establishment has also been able to justify its self-perpetuating rule to the people of Pakistan. Similarly, when dealing with the international community, the military government has often portrayed itself as the best defender against the same extremist groups that it has done so much to nurture—an effort somewhat akin to the old tale of the man who murdered his wife and then pleaded for leniency as a widower. . . .

The Power of Religious Parties

For Pakistan itself, Musharraf's plan—outlined in an address to the nation this month—signals an end to a quarter century in which political power has flowed gradually yet steadily in the direction of conservative religious forces, turning the country into a safe haven for extremists.

Los Angeles Times
29 January 2002

Most fundamentalist religious parties in Pakistan have never developed broad support at the ballot box on those occasions when citizens have been allowed to freely express their will. The two most powerful political parties remain the Pakistan People's Party and the Muslim League. Election results during Pakistan's ten-year experiment with democracy belie alarmist claims that Islamic extremists are on the verge of taking over the state, and the military is the last defence. Periods of representative rule have, in fact, strengthened moderate democratic forces, not their religious counterparts.

By 1988, when General Zia-ul-Haq's demise in a mid-air explosion ended over a decade of military rule, state patronage had given Islamic extremist organisations considerable political clout. But when Pakistani citizens were permitted to elect their own representatives, they voted overwhelmingly for moderate, mainstream secular parties. Electoral support for extremist religious parties, in fact, progressively declined between 1988 and 1999.

The rise of the Taliban in Afghanistan in the 1990s, had, for instance, stimulated fears that their success would be replicated in Pakistan. Support for parties such as the Jamiat-Ulema-e-Islam (led by Fazlur Rehman) (JUI-F), one of those that had helped the military to create and sustain the Taliban, however, has been minuscule in every national election. In 1988, the JUI-F obtained seven national assembly seats with 1.84 per cent of total votes; in 1990, six seats with 2.94 per cent of votes; in 1993, four seats with 2.4 per cent of the vote; and, in 1997, only 2 seats with 1.61 per cent of the votes. Ironically in the 1997 elections, when its Taliban allies had captured 90 per cent of Afghanistan's territory, the JUI-F was soundly defeated in its Northwest Frontier stronghold by the Muslim League and failed to win a single seat. . . .

A Fundamental Strategic Shift?

Musharraf is now in the Ataturk position, a dictator deploying absolute power for the apparently paradoxical ends of modernising and democratising. Like Ataturk, he has to work in chaotic conditions to create a nation state capable of dealing with the difficulties it faces. He made his existential choice when he broke with the Taliban, joined the American coalition, and opened local air bases to American aircraft. He has also purged senior generals in the army and the ISI who were Islamists and promoters of the "strategic depth" doctrine that has wreaked such havoc. He has banned Jaish-e-Muhammad and Lashkar-e-Taiba and several other terror groups as well, closing 500 of their offices and ordering the tracking of their funds with the aim of freezing them. In the most fraught part of this U-turn, he has had arrested an estimated 2,000 militants who until now were secretly subsidised and encouraged by the ISI. He describes madrassahs correctly as places that 'propagate hatred and violence,' and in the future they will have to register with the authorities and teach modern courses. Rival politicians and influential opinion-makers who hitherto have criticised Musharraf for usurping democratic rule are now coming around to him because Pakistan has changed course and will not become an extremist Islamist state.

The National Review
25 February 2002

The government of Pakistan has taken a number of important steps in recent months, including sharply curtailing its direct support for the Taliban, widely making its bases available for allied forces, shifting its rhetoric, clamping down on public fundraising by extremist groups, banning several of the most notorious Islamic extremist groups and detaining a significant number of militants. While on the surface it is easy to portray this as a 180-degree policy turn, this claim bears closer analysis. Indeed, it remains to be seen whether the moves amount to a fundamental strategic shift or rather simply a series of tactical moves designed to curry favour with the West while maintaining the military's dominant position.

In several areas, there is far less change then meets the eye. First, the military government was the over-arching institution in Pakistan's public life before 11 September, and despite modest moves, it appears the October 2002 election will be so heavily engineered as to constitute only a veneer of a genuinely competitive electoral process. Already the government has widely curtailed the eligibility of potential candidates, added a substantial number of parliamentary seats for "technocrats" that it hopes to control and stacked the high courts. Through selective accountability, Musharraf is attempting to eliminate his civilian rivals. Sentenced to life imprisonment for hijacking Musharraf's plane at the time of the coup, former Prime Minister Sharif has been exiled to Saudi Arabia. Cases have been instituted to prevent Bhutto from running.

At the same time, Musharraf has created an alternative civilian clientele through nominal local bodies and by encouraging the break up of the Muslim League. The splinter group of the latter, the Muslim League (Quaid-i-Azam), headed by former Punjab Governor Mian Mohammad Azhar, is more than likely to receive governmental patronage during the elections. Since Musharraf has also appointed a pliant Election Commissioner, former Supreme Court Chief Justice Irshad Hussain Khan, it is equally unlikely that the election commission will question or curb malpractice.

General Musharraf is well on the way to acquiring an additional five-year presidential term virtually by military fiat. He has openly told local political leaders that he would like to serve an additional five-year term after that—giving him at least thirteen years of uncontested military rule. This contrasts sharply with his comments in October 1999 after he assumed power when he assured the nation and the world, "The armed forces have no intention to stay in charge any longer than is absolutely necessary to pave the way for true democracy to flourish in Pakistan." Musharraf has also revealed his intention to restore the president's power to dismiss the prime minister and dissolve the legislature. Further, by establishing a potential military-dominated National Security Council with de facto veto over the actions of an elected prime minister and parliament, military officials are seeking to ensure control over Pakistan's government in perpetuity.

It would appear to be no coincidence that the military is pushing through these extra-constitutional measures when its international standing is at a high water mark because of its cooperation with the anti-terrorism campaign. Senior Pakistani officials have acknowledged off the record that they have been told directly by the Bush administration that Washington would prefer to see General Musharraf remain in power for a number of years. If true, it would constitute extraordinarily poor judgement to endorse what must be considered a military dictatorship over a legitimate democratic process. That choice can be shown almost always to result in more instability, not less, over the long term. Pakistan has never been able to develop full civilian control over its military. The fact that it has fought three wars with India since Independence while failing to make much needed investments in public education and health underscores the high cost of marginalising the country's civilian leadership.

Kashmir and Afghanistan

The events of 11 September also appear to have done little to fundamentally shift the Pakistani military's approach to Kashmir despite tactical adjustments. After the 13 December 2001 terrorist attack on the Indian parliament and the large Indian military build-up on the Line of Control, Pakistan appears to have curtailed its support for cross border raids by "Jihadi" groups. However, given the close scrutiny by both India and the United States to activities across the

Line of Control, this appears more expediency than good will and not real abandonment of proxy war. President Musharraf has repeatedly made it clear publicly that Pakistan will not lessen its commitment to the cause of Kashmir. Addressing gatherings on Kashmir Solidarity Day on 5 February 2002, he condemned India for attempting to "mislead the world community by projecting the indigenous struggle of the Kashmiri people as terrorists", and reiterated Pakistan's diplomatic, political and moral support for "their struggle that includes the blood of thousands of martyrs".

It would be no surprise if the ISI continues to support insurgent groups both in Kashmir and elsewhere in India with funds and intelligence while reducing cross border raids. Indeed, there are some indications on the ground that Pakistan is moving in this direction. Such an approach would maintain the larger Pakistani strategy to bleed India as a means either to achieve a favourable settlement on Kashmir or "internationalise" the conflict. Continuing to embrace such a strategy would only ensure that tensions with India are maintained, hobbling Pakistan's prospects for economic and social development.

Similarly, only time will tell if the ISI and Pakistan's military can approach Afghanistan with relative restraint. . . . A long history of meddling in Afghan affairs has most often proved counterproductive and left Islamabad with an unstable neighbour and host to millions of refugees. While Pakistan has been far from alone in pursuing such ill-advised policies in Afghanistan, it has often suffered the most as a result. This again highlights the dangers of having the military and intelligence services act without a civilian brake on their foreign policy activities.

Lastly, amid suggestions that the military and intelligence services do not wish to alienate fringe parties as the electoral process is manipulated in the run-up to October [scheduled elections of 2002], there continue to be serious questions regarding the scale to which Musharraf has actually cracked down on extremist groups. There are few indications that the military government has made a serious attempt to reform the madrassas system or to push through core changes in its curricula. On the contrary, a number of government officials continue to make highly supportive statements to officials running these religious schools, and efforts to develop educational alternatives have seen little progress. In fact, the military government lauds the social and economic contributions made by religious seminaries, denies it intends to crack down on them and emphasises that it is aiming only at ending sectarian terrorism. "Western countries either lack information or lack sincerity about madaris", noted Musharraf's Minister for Religious Affairs, Dr. Mehamood Ahmad Ghazi, who also categorically claimed, "It is absolutely clear that no religious school is involved in the training of terrorists".

The murder of *Wall Street Journal* correspondent Daniel Pearl by Jaish-I-Mohammad activists and sectarian killings of Shias by Sunni terrorists are hardly evidence of government success in reining in extremists. The government needs to take immediate steps to identify and close down madrassas that give military training to religious extremists. Those responsible for propagating religious hate and for terror acts must be arrested and tried in courts of law. But jihadis will continue to flourish if the state and its intelligence agencies support their activities in Afghanistan or Kashmir. . . .

The Military Must Be Stopped

A strong, secure and stable Pakistan will need to be built on a far more robust economy, aggressive efforts to educate a population where more than 50 per cent of students drop out by the American equivalent of the third grade, establishing the rule of law and unshackling a robust civil society that can combat pervasive corruption. All these efforts will demand resources and need to be supported by the public. However, as long as Pakistan's military and intelligence services continue to claim the lion's share of the national budget—official estimates are at least 29 per cent, with actual figures likely much higher—it is difficult to believe that Pakistan will be able to meet its challenges.

As the single wealthiest, most powerful and influential institution in Pakistan, whose generals receive generous perks on a regular basis, the military is unlikely to limit its own broad reach voluntarily. Indeed, it is remarkable that generous U.S. assistance will flow to a country where the large military budget is approved only as a single line item by the parliament—a lack of transparency that encourages corruption as fundamental in the military establishment as in any of Pakistan's other institutions.

It is also difficult to think that Pakistan's military will make a good faith effort to resolve its myriad of tensions with India, when those have often been used as the prime justification by the military for its over-arching domestic role. Very few institutions would embrace any peace agreement that would seem to ensure their own increasing marginalisation, which provides all the more reason for the international community to put pressure on Pakistan to achieve an actual democracy rather than simply its veneer.

There continues to be tremendous thirst and demand for genuine democracy in Pakistan, a remarkable fact given the travails that the country has experienced. While the notion of "managed democracy" may appeal both to the generals in Pakistan and to the short term interests of western planners, the deep, systematic and institutional challenges that face Pakistan will only be surmounted when the country has a competitive and fair political process that allows the will of the people to be heard.

Periodical Bibliography

The following articles have been selected to supplement the diverse views presented in this chapter.

Assam Sajjad Akhtar — "'Gujarat' and the Pakistani State," *Himal South Asian*, April 2002. www.himalmag.com.

Ajay Behera — "Pakistan's Dilemma," *Hindu*, May 22, 2002. www.hinduonnet.com/thehindu.

Darryl D'Monte — "Demographic Fatigue in India," *New Leader*, July 2000.

Celia W. Dugger — "Religious Riots Loom over Indian Politics," *New York Times*, July 27, 2002.

Economist — "Unproductive," September 6, 2001.

James Flanigan — "Business Is a Must for India, Pakistan," *Los Angeles Times*, January 2, 2002.

H.D.S. Greenway — "Hindu Nationalism Clouds the Face of India," *World Policy Journal*, April 1, 2001.

Robert E. Litan — "The Internet Economy," *Foreign Policy*, March 1, 2001.

Lancy Lobo — "Religion and Politics in India," *America*, February 19, 2000.

Julian Manyon — "The 2,500 Years' War," *Spectator*, March 9, 2002. www.spectator.co.uk.

Tyler Marshall — "Asia's New Hotbed of Moderation," *Los Angeles Times*, January 29, 2002.

Pankaj Mishra — "Hinduism's Political Resurgence," *New York Times*, February 25, 2002.

Ron Moreau and Zahid Hussain — "Power and Privilege: Life Is Tough in Pakistan, for Everybody but the Generals," *Newsweek*, October 14, 2002.

Alex Ninian — "Hindu and Muslim Strife in India," *Contemporary Review*, June 2002.

Ahmed Rashid — "Pakistan on the Edge," *New York Review of Books*, October 10, 2002. www.nybooks.com.

Arundhati Roy — "Fascism's Firm Footprint in India," *Nation*, September 30, 2002.

Geeta Vaidyanathan — "In Gandhi's Footsteps," *Alternatives Journal*, Spring 2002.

Geoffrey C. Ward — "India," *National Geographic*, May 1997.

For Further Discussion

Chapter 1

1. Anne Applebaum suggests that it is "borderline racist" to argue that people in India and Pakistan are more likely to start a nuclear war than Europeans and Americans because they do not have a full comprehension of such a war's destructiveness. Do you agree or disagree with her assessment? Is there evidence for or against such prejudice in the viewpoints by Sam Gardiner and Praful Bidwai?

2. Matthew Parris argues that removing all nuclear weapons from South Asia would leave the region a more dangerous place. Praful Bidwai asserts that nuclear abolition is a necessary first step to regional security. What is the main difference in these authors' reasoning that leads them to these opposite conclusions?

3. Muqtedar Khan urges U.S. intervention between India and Pakistan while Charles Glass advocates action by the United Nations. Could both pathways of action be pursued, or is one in conflict with the other? Explain your answer.

Chapter 2

1. Do James P. Lucier's arguments on the status of India's ethnic/religious minority groups rest on the assumption that the only choices for such groups are either independence or oppression? Defend your answer citing parts of the viewpoint.

2. Asghar Ali Engineer argues that India's constitution may serve as a model for other countries in protecting minority rights. After reading his article, and that of Lucier, do you agree or disagree? Defend your answer.

3. Francois Gautier argues that Christians have often mistreated or persecuted Hindus in the past. Do you believe this to be a relevant or convincing argument concerning the treatment of Christians by Hindus in the present, as described by Jeff M. Sellers? Why or why not?

4. Assume that you were appointed by the United Nations to convene new negotiations to settle the Kashmir question. After reading the three viewpoints on Kashmir, what ideas do you have on how to resolve the dispute? What concessions, if any, would you demand of the disputants? What additional information do you believe you must have? Explain your answers.

Chapter 3

1. Melissa Dell argues that the United States should regard Pakistan as an ally in the war against terrorism. In contrast, Leon Hadar maintains that Pakistan has a reputation for aiding terrorists and should not be trusted. Examine the evidence that both authors provide to make their arguments. Which author do you find more convincing and why?

2. Victor M. Gobarev, Larry M. Wortzel, and Dana R. Dillon disagree on whether or not India's possession of nuclear weapons threatens U.S. security. Gobarev contends that accepting India as a nuclear power would be the best way to guarantee stability in Southeast Asia, which would ultimately benefit America's homeland security. In contrast, Wortzel and Dillon argue that the United States should demand that India dismantle its nuclear weapons because they jeopardize America's security. Taking into account the evidence that the authors provide to support their views, do you think that India's nuclear weapons are a threat to the United States? What stance would you recommend the United States take in regard to India's nuclear arms?

3. Shishir Thadani agrees with Human Rights Watch that India's caste system is a serious problem. However, Thadani disagrees with the organization about the role the international community should take in addressing the problem. He claims that since other nations perpetuated discrimination during colonial times, they should do more than condemn India's caste system. Instead, Western nations should encourage poor Indians to immigrate to their countries. In your opinion, is Thadani's suggestion practical or desirable? Make sure to reference Thadani's argument while developing your answer.

Chapter 4

1. What statistics and trends do Lester R. Brown and Brian Halweil cite in arguing that India's future is unpromising? Compare them to the facts and trends emphasized by Prasenjit Basu. What sort of facts and statistics (economic, social, environmental) do you believe are most important in assessing the future of a nation? Defend your answer.

2. Both Gurcharan Das and Vandana Shiva argue that globalization and free trade are transforming India but differ in opinion about whether these transformations are good or bad for its people. Do their disagreements stem from factual disagreement on how exactly India is changing, or do they originate in value disagree-

ments as to what constitutes good change and bad change? Explain your answer with examples from the viewpoints.

3. Arun R. Swamy compares Hindu nationalism to fascism. What evidence does he use to support his serious charge? Can evidence for or against Swamy's charges of fascism be found in the articles by David Frawley and Sarita Sarvate? Explain.

4. David Pryce-Jones argues that the threat of Islamic fundamentalism is serious enough to justify military dictatorship. The International Crisis Group plays down the threat and influence that Islamic fundamentalists have in Pakistan, arguing that the military itself poses the greatest threat to Pakistan's future. After reading these viewpoints, which do you believe makes the strongest argument? Explain.

Organizations to Contact

The editors have compiled the following list of organizations concerned with the issues debated in this book. The descriptions are derived from materials provided by the organizations. All have publications or information available for interested readers. The list was compiled on the date of publication of the present volume; the information provided here may change. Be aware that many organizations take several weeks or longer to respond to inquiries, so allow as much time as possible.

Amnesty International (AI)
International Secretariat
1 Easton St., London WC1X 0DW, United Kingdom
e-mail: amnestyis@amnesty.org • website: www.amnesty.org

Amnesty International is a worldwide campaigning movement that works to promote internationally recognized human rights. It has published articles on India and Pakistan in its quarterly newsletter *Amnesty Action*, as well as made available reports and briefings on the two nations on its website.

Arms Control Association (ACA)
1726 M St. NW, Washington, DC 20036
(202) 463-8270 • fax: (202) 463-8273
e-mail: aca@armscontrol.org • website: www.armscontrol.org

The ACA is a national membership organization that works to educate the public and promote effective arms control policies. It publishes the magazine *Arms Control Today*. Documents and articles on nuclear weapons in India and Pakistan can be found on its website.

Brookings Institution
1775 Massachusetts Ave. NW, Washington, DC 20036
(202) 797-6000 • fax: (202) 797-6004
e-mail: brookinfo@brook.edu • website: www.brookings.org

The institution, founded in 1927, is a think tank that conducts research and education in foreign policy, economics, government, and the social sciences. It established the India/South Asia Project in 1998 to conduct and disseminate research on this region and American foreign policy implications. Its publications include the quarterly *Brookings Review*, periodic *Policy Briefs*, and books including *India: Emerging Power*.

Center for Strategic and International Studies (CSIS)

1800 K St. NW, Suite 400, Washington, DC 20006
(202) 887-0200 • fax: (202) 775-3199
website: www.csis.org

The center works to provide world leaders with strategic insights and policy options on current and emerging global issues. It publishes the *South Asian Monitor*, a monthly newsletter on events in the region, the *Washington Quarterly*, a journal on political, economic, and security issues, and other publications, including reports that can be downloaded from its website.

Center for the Advanced Study of India

University of Pennsylvania
3833 Chestnut St., Suite 130, Philadelphia, PA 19104-3106
(215) 898-6247 • fax: (215) 573-2595
e-mail: casi@sas.upenn.edu • website: www.sas.upenn.edu/casi

Founded in 1992, the center is the only institute in the United States dedicated to the study of contemporary India. Its sponsors research projects and disseminate information through its publications, including the journal *Doing Business in India*. Reports and papers are available on its website.

Embassy of India

2107 Massachusetts Ave. NW, Washington DC 20008
(202) 939-7000 • fax: (202) 265-4351
e-mail: info2@indiagov.org • website: www.indianembassy.org

In addition to providing consular services, the embassy handles requests for general information on India. Reference documents, policy statements, and speeches by Indian government officials, and selections from Indian newspapers can all be found on its website.

Hoover Institution

Stanford University, Stanford, CA 94305-6010
(650) 723-1754 • fax: (650) 723-1687
website: www-hoover.stanford.edu

The Hoover Institution is a public policy research center devoted to advanced study of politics, economics, and political economy—both domestic and foreign—as well as international affairs. It publishes the quarterly *Hoover Digest*, which occasionally includes articles on India and Pakistan, as well as a newsletter and special reports.

Human Rights Watch (HRW)

485 Fifth Ave., New York, NY 10017-6104
(212) 972-8400 • fax: (212) 972-0905
e-mail: hrwnyc@hrw.org • website: www.hrw.org

Human Rights Watch regularly investigates human rights abuses in over seventy countries around the world, including India and Pakistan. Its goal is to hold governments accountable for human rights violations they commit against individuals because of their political, ethnic, or religious affiliations. HRW publishes the *Human Rights Watch Quarterly* newsletter, the annual *Human Rights Watch World Report*, and a semiannual publications catalog.

Jammu and Kashmir Council for Human Rights (JKCHR)

PO Box 241, London SW17 9LJ, United Kingdom
440 208 640 8630 • fax: 440 208 640 8546
e-mail: infor@jkchr.com • website: www.jkchr.com

JKCHR is a nongovernmental organization that performs relief work and monitors human rights conditions in the Indian state of Jammu and Kashmir. Numerous reports and statements are available on its website.

United States Department of State, Bureau of South Asian Affairs

U.S. Department of State
2201 C St. NW, Washington, DC 20520
(202) 647-4000
e-mail: secretary@state.gov • website: www.state.gov/p/eap

The bureau deals with U.S. foreign policy and U.S. relations with the countries in the South Asia region, including India and Pakistan. Its website offers country information as well as news briefings and press statements on U.S. foreign policy.

Websites

Dawn, the Internet Edition

www.dawn.com

This website is the online edition of the leading English-language newspaper in Pakistan.

Expressindia.com

www.expressindia.com

The website includes articles from the *Indian Express* and *Financial Express* newspapers.

Good News India

www.goodnewsindia.com

This website features articles from India that emphasize positive developments and trends.

The Hindu

www.hinduonnet.com

The website feature articles and editorials from one of India's leading newspapers.

Islamic Republic of Pakistan Official Website

www.pak.gov.pk

This official website of the Pakistani government includes a profile of President Musharraf as well as the text of his speeches.

Bibliography of Books

Stephen Alter — *Amritsar to Lahore: A Journey Across the India-Pakistan Border*. Philadelphia: University of Pennsylvania Press, 2000.

Gary K. Bertsch, Seema Gahlaut, and Anupam Srivastava, eds. — *Engaging India: U.S. Strategic Relations with the World's Largest Democracy*. London, UK: Routledge, 1999.

Chetan Bhatt — *Hindu Nationalism: Origins, Ideologies, and Modern Myths*. New York: Berg, 2001.

Praful Bidwai and Achin Vanaik — *New Nukes: India, Pakistan, and Global Disarmament*. Oxford, UK: Signal Books, 2000.

Steven Cohen — *India: Emerging Power*. Washington, DC: Brookings Institution, 2001.

Stuart Corbridge and John Harriss — *Reinventing India: Liberalisation, Hindu Nationalism, and Popular Democracy*. Cambridge, UK: Polity Press, 2000.

Gurcharan Das — *India Unbound*. New York: Alfred A. Knopf, 2001.

Sumit Ganguly — *Conflict Unending: India-Pakistan Tensions Since 1947*. New York: Columbia University Press, 2002.

William Goodwin — *India*. San Diego: Lucent Books, 2000.

William Goodwin — *Pakistan*. San Diego: Lucent Books, 2003.

Selig S. Harrison, Paul H. Kreisberg, and Dennis Kux, eds. — *India and Pakistan: The First Fifty Years*. Washington, DC: Woodrow Wilson Center Press, 1999.

David Haslam — *Caste Out! The Liberation Struggle of the Dalits in India*. London, UK: CTBI, 1999.

Ronald B. Inden — *Imagining India*. Bloomington: Indiana University Press, 2001.

Christophe Jaffrelot, ed. — *Pakistan: Nationalism Without a Nation?* London, UK: Zed Books, 2002.

Pramila Jayapal — *Pilgrimage: One Woman's Return to a Changing India*. Seattle, WA: Seal Press, 2000.

Laura D. Jenkins — *Identity and Identification in India: Defining the Disadvantaged*. London, UK: RoutledgeCurzon, 2003.

Rob Jenkins — *Democratic Politics and Economic Reform in India*. New York: Cambridge University Press, 1999.

Dwijendra Narayan Jha — *The Myth of the Holy Cow*. New York: Verso, 2002.

Owen Bennett Jones   *Pakistan: The Eye of the Storm*. New Haven, CT: Yale University Press, 2002.

Sangeeta Kamat   *Development Hegemony: NGOs and the State in India*. New York: Oxford University Press, 2002.

Hiranmay Karlekar, ed.   *Independent India: The First Fifty Years*. New York: Oxford University Press, 1998.

Sunil Khilnani   *The Idea of India*. New York: Farrar, Straus, and Giroux, 1997.

Kim Knott   *Hinduism: A Very Short Introduction*. New York: Oxford University Press, 2000.

Atul Kohli, ed.   *The Success of India's Democracy*. Princeton, NJ: Princeton University Press, 2001.

Smitu Kothari and Zia Mian, eds.   *Out of the Nuclear Shadow*. London, UK: Zed Books, 2001.

Dennis Kux   *The United States and Pakistan, 1947–2000: Disenchanted Allies*. Washington, DC: Woodrow Wilson Center, 2001.

Victoria Schofield   *Kashmir in Conflict: India, Pakistan, and the Unfinished War*. New York: I.B.Tauris, 2000.

Ghanshyam Shah, ed.   *Dalit Identity and Politics*. New Delhi, India: Sage Publications India, 2001.

Rajeev Sharma   *Pak Proxy War: A Story of ISI, bin Laden, and Kargil*. New Delhi, India: Kaveri Books, 1999.

Shalendra D. Sharma   *Development and Democracy in India*. Boulder, CO: Lynne Rienner, 1999.

Pamela Shurmer-Smith   *India: Globalization and Change*. London: Arnold, 2000.

Mysore Marasimhachar Srinivas   *Collected Essays*. New York: Oxford University Press, 2002.

Hilary Synott   *The Causes and Consequences of South Asia's Nuclear Tests*. New York: Oxford University Press, 2000.

Ian Talbot   *Inventing the Nation: India and Pakistan*. New York: Oxford University Press, 2000.

Shashi Taroor   *India: From Midnight to the Millennium*. New York: Arcade, 1997.

Ashutosh Varshney   *Ethnic Conflict and Civic Life: Hindus and Muslims in India*. New Haven, CT: Yale University Press, 2002.

Heather Lehr Wagner   *India and Pakistan*. Broomall, PA: Chelsea House, 2002.

Mary Anne Weaver

Pakistan: In the Shadow of Jihad and Afghanistan. New York: Farrar, Straus, and Giroux, 2002.

Anita M. Weiss and
S. Zulfiger Gilani, eds.

Power and Civil Society in Pakistan. New York: Oxford University Press, 2001.

Robert G. Wirsing

India, Pakistan, and the Kashmir Dispute: On Regional Conflict and Its Resolution. New York: Palgrave Macmillan, 1997.

John Zavos

The Emergence of Hindu Nationalism in India. New York: Oxford University Press, 2000.

Index

215